Access America Guide Series

ACCESS AMERICA
GUIDE TO THE
WESTERN NATIONAL PARKS

An Atlas and Guide for Visitors with Disabilities

NORTHERN CARTOGRAPHIC

WEIDENFELD & NICOLSON
New York

Published by Weidenfeld & Nicolson, New York
A Division of Wheatland Corporation
841 Broadway
New York, New York 10003-4793

Published in Canada by General Publishing Company, Ltd.

The phrase "Access America" is the trademarked slogan of the United States Architectural and Transportation Barriers Compliance Board (ATBCB). The publisher wishes to disclaim any relationship or affiliation with this federal agency. The use of this trademarked phrase, in the title of the publication, does not indicate or imply any endorsement of this publication or its information by this federal agency.

Library of Congress Cataloging-in-Publication Data

Access America guide to the western national parks; an atlas and guide for visitors with disabilities / Northern Cartographic. — 1st ed.

    p.   cm.
   ISBN 1-55584-401-4
    1. National parks and reserves—Pacific States—Guide-books.   2. Pacific States—Description and travel—1981-   —Guide-books.   3. Parks and the handicapped—Pacific States.   4. Handicapped—Travel—Pacific States—Guide-books.   I. Northern Cartographic, Inc. II.   Title: Guide to the western national parks.
E160.A29   1988
917.94—dc20   89-9142
                                   CIP

Printed in Italy by New Interlitho S.p.A. - Milan
This book is printed on acid-free paper
First Edition
10 9 8 7 6 5 4 3 2 1

Also available: *Access America Guide to the Eastern National Parks, Access America Guide to the Rocky Mountain National Parks, Access America Guide to the Southwestern National Parks.*

Table of Contents

Legend

Highways

——————(75)—————— Interstate Highway

——————(180)—————— U.S. Highway

——————(16)—————— State Highway

——————(89)—————— State Highway

– – – – – – – – – Gravel or Dirt Road

Road Elevations

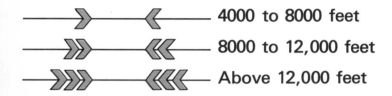

——— 4000 to 8000 feet

——— 8000 to 12,000 feet

——— Above 12,000 feet

The following symbols appear on the **Medical and Support Services** maps.

H   Hospital

W   Wheelchair Sales or Repair

P   Prosthetics and Orthotics

O   Therapeutic Oxygen

D   Dialysis

V   Veterinarian

GRAND JUNCTION   A city which offers all six services listed above.

The following symbols represent park places, facilities and features in the National Parks. Color represents the level of accessibility.

▮ Accessible

▮ Usable, Accessible with Assistance or Reported to be Accessible

▮ Not Accessible

Museum
Museum
Museum   Name of Place

Restroom, Women

Restroom, Men

R R R   Restrooms (park map)

Water

Telephone

V V V   Vista

T T T   Picnic Table

Self-Guiding Trail

Trail

Amphitheater

Clinic or Hospital

Campground

Parking

? ? ?   Information

•••••••••• Route of Travel

 Administrative or Personnel Areas in Visitor Centers.

For a complete explanation of symbols and terms, please refer to the introduction.

Foreword

Outdoor recreation experiences are one of life's highlights. For me, these experiences have always been a tremendous source of personal rejuvenation and refreshment. It is unfortunate that the potential for these experiences is, in general, more limited for persons with disabilities than for non-disabled persons. This situation holds true even in our national parks, those special places designated to be the shared heritage of all Americans.

Compounding the lack of actual access has been the lack of clear and accurate information about "accessibility." Many times I have telephoned sites or read guides that have labeled places "accessible," only to find when I arrived, that there were accessible parking spaces or an accessible toilet, but no way to enter the nature center or picnic area or campground, nothing available in large print, and no telecommunication device for deaf persons.

Although there is a long way to go before equal opportunity for people of all levels of ability is achieved, things are changing. The national parks, in particular, have been responsive to the growing recognition of this need.

It was only several months ago that I was pleased to write the foreword to the award-winning parent publication of these Access America guides. Since that time, Access America: An Atlas and Guide to the National Parks for Visitors with Disabilities has become the object of much critical acclaim and has seen wide distribution to libraries and professional organizations around the country. It is a very exciting prospect that regional selections from that unique reference will now be available at the local bookstore in this Access America Guide Series.

The authors of Access America have demonstrated a remarkable awareness and understanding of the difficulties, both natural and man-made, faced by persons with disabilities. The final product is a testament to the rigorous process, including extensive surveys and site visits, employed to develop this series and the many years spent laying its groundwork.

Fifteen years ago the majority of accessible features described in these guides did not exist. The fact that progress has been made means that persons with disabilities have gained and are continuing to gain access to more opportunities.

I believe that all Americans, whether disabled or not, have the right to experience recreation and have access to recreation facilities and spaces. I commend the National Park Service for its initiatives to make the out-of-doors accessible to persons with disabilities.

I applaud the efforts of Northern Cartographic, Inc. to create a resource that will greatly enhance the outdoor recreation experiences of persons with disabilities and their families and friends. The interest, curiosity, and commitment demonstrated by the authors are exemplary.

Lex Frieden
Executive Director, TIRR Foundation, and
Assistant Professor, Baylor College of Medicine

Preface

Welcome to the *Access America Guide Series* on the national parks. It is our highest hope that the use of this long overdue and, in most respects, unique guide and atlas series will substantially enrich your next visit to some of our country's most treasured resources.

The concept of an atlas/guide to the national parks, specifically designed for visitors with disabilities, occurred in 1983. The idea took root in our professional backgrounds in geography and cartography as well as our personal travel experiences with family members. It was timely, coming in the midst of over a decade of progress in both attitudinal and physical changes which impacted directly on the "accessibility" of the parks themselves.

Communicating the nature and location of "access" is in large part a geographic statement and its ideal medium is *the map*. Although we felt well qualified to handle the graphic and technical aspects of the problems involved in this undertaking, a professional background in health and disability was conspicuously lacking. As the project evolved, this deficit was easily overcome.

Perhaps it was because of the inherent excitement of producing such an unparalleled atlas, or the generous spirit which characterizes many of the professionals in the health/disability field; whatever the reason, the five-hundred letters we sent out to recruit assistance with the project resulted in the creation of a talent pool of more than sixty individuals with backgrounds representing nearly all aspects of health and disability.

The response from the National Park Service was no less phenomenal. From our very first inquiry to the Park Service's Washington Office of Special Programs and Populations, through the myriad telephone calls to various Park Service agencies, to the numerous park personnel who labored through our intensive series of questionnaires, all greeted the idea with enthusiasm, energy and commitment.

The recent publication of our 464-page library reference, *Access America: An Atlas and Guide to the National Parks for Visitors with Disabilities*, culminated some five years of research and production, and has since received much critical acclaim. The travel series, now in hand, is based on a selected regional breakdown of this larger publication and fulfills our original committment to make this information available beyond the confines of libraries and professional organizations.

If we have succeeded in the purposes of producing these much needed guides, it is because of the generosity and cooperative efforts of hundreds of individuals, including many park visitors with disabilities, whose intellectual and material contributions have made this series a reality.

For all these people and for Northern Cartographic,

Peter Shea, Edward Antczak, Laura Feaster

Burlington, Vermont

Acknowledgments

Although Northern Cartographic claims exclusive responsibility for the nature, content and format of this atlas series (including any shortcomings), we have had considerable assistance in its research and production. The authors wish to acknowledge a number of individuals who gave generously and without reservation of their time, effort and expertise in the service of this project. It is no exaggeration to say that without their input completion of this series would have been impossible. Included in this group of exceptional people are: **Kay Ellis**, Recreation Specialist, National Park Service; **Franz Stillfried**, Information Coordinator/Advocate; **Steve Stone**, Access Coordinator, National Park Service; **Burt Wallrich**, Total Access Camping; **Erica Garfin**, Vermont Center for Independent Living; **Phyllis Cangemi**, Whole Access Project; **Meg Graf**, Spokes Unlimited.

Also **David Gaines**, National Park Service; **Nora Griffin-Shirley**, University of Arkansas at Little Rock; **Jim Tuck**, National Park Service; **Michael Warshawsky**, Access Advocate; **Ray Bloomer**, Disability Program Specialist, National Park Service; **Robert E. Michaels**, Arizona Bridge to Independent Living; **Ron Hanson**, Maine Governor's Committee on the Employment of the Handicapped; **Heidi Ann Johnson**, Ohio State University; **Jerry Duncan**, SCILL (Tours/Travel).

Also **Marianne J. Cashatt**, Woodrow Wilson Rehabilitation Center; **Robert M. Montague**, Special Olympics; **Colleen Trout** and **James Beck**, Challenge Alaska; **Helen Hecker**, Publisher/Writer; **Ray Cheever**, Accent on Living Magazine; **William G.B. Graham, M.D.**, University of Vermont; **Dale Brown**, National Network of Learning-Disabled Adults; **Mariam Brownson**, L.T.D. Travel; **Dolores A. Black**, Bowling Green State University.

Also **Peter Axelson**, Beneficial Designs; **Willie Cashin**, Woodrow Wilson Center for Independent Living; **Brent K. Askvig**, North Dakota Association for Persons with Severe Handicaps.

Although we are indebted to perhaps hundreds of individuals who in some fashion assisted us in our research, we are obliged to cite a number of contributors who were especially helpful in making this series a reality. They include: **John A. Nesbitt**, Special Recreation Inc.; **G. Andrew Fleming**, Paralyzed Veterans of America; **Dennis C. Almasy**, Access Specialist; **Dr.** and **Mrs. Samuel Genensky**, Center for the Partially Sighted; **Ruth Hall-Phillips**, Paralyzed Veterans of America; **Ismael S. Paredes**, California Governor's Committee for Employment of the Handicapped; **Chryss Jones**, Vermont Center for Independent Living; **Dr. Diana Richardson**, University of Maryland.

Also **Robert S. Zywicki**, The Itinerary Magazine; **Dr. Ronald J. Anderson**, University of Northern Iowa; **Gary W. Olsen**, National Association of the Deaf; **Merton J. Gilliam**, Rehabilitation Services Administration, Government of the District of Columbia; **Alton Hodges**, National Institute of Handicapped Research; **Ann Bowman**, National Park Service; **Nina M. Hill**, International Center for the Disabled.

Also **John Kopchik Jr.**, Disabled Outdoors; **Sharon Schleich**, Flying Wheels Travel; **Vicki Cook**, Goodwill Rehabilitation Inc.; **Barry Corbet**, Access Inc.; **Frank J. Deckert**, National Park Service; **Judith M. Dixon**, National Library Service for the Blind and Physically Handicapped.

Also **Robert Gorski**, President's Committee on the Employment of the Handicapped; **Marge Hadley**, Michigan Chapter, National Arthritis Foundation; **Dennis L. Heath**, State of Oregon; **Rosemarie Kasper**, Vocational Rehabilitation Counselor; **Robert B. Kasparek**, National Park Service; **Fred Marcus**, national park visitor; **E.C. Keller**, Foundation for Science and the Handicapped.

Also **Stuart R. Mace**, National Easter Seal Society; **Lorraine Marchi**, National Association for the Visually Handicapped; **Roberta Stein**, Barrier Free Alaska; and, **Syd Jacobs**, national park visitor.

National Park Service

For general support and research assistance we would like to thank David C. Park, Chief, and Thomas Coleman, Recreation Specialist, Special Programs and Populations Branch; David E. Gackenbach, Chief, Concessions Division; Warren H. Hill, Associate Regional Director of Operations, Midwest Region; Jody Notch, Technical Information Assistant, Denver Service Center; Edie Ramey, Chief, Technical Information Center, Denver Service Center; Ann Wazenski, Special Programs and Populations Branch; and, Ricardo Lewis, Public Relations.

We are deeply indebted to all the park personnel who took direct responsibility for responding to our lengthy and tedious questionnaires, and subsequently reviewing the text. These include: **John Palmer** and **Larry Waldron**, Chief Park Interpreters, Sequoia and Kings Canyon N.P.'s; **Richard Vance**, Chief Park Naturalist, Lassen Volcanic N.P.; **Lloyd 'Smitty' Parrat**, Special Populations Coordinator and **Larry Frederick**, East District Naturalist, Olympic N.P.; **Don Fox**, Park Landscape Architect, Yosemite N.P.; **Henry Tanski**, Assistant Chief of Interpretation, Crater Lake N.P.; **John Cabral**, Redwood N.P.; and, **Loren E. Lane**, Access Coordinator, Mt. Rainier N.P.

National Park Superintendents

We wish to acknowledge the enthusiastic and committed cooperation we received from the individual park superintendents. Their strong support of our efforts allowed full, active participation by the staff they supervise. Our gratitude is extended to Gilbert Blinn, Lassen Volcanic N.P.; Douglas Warnock, Redwood N.P.; John Davis, Sequoia and Kings Canyon N.P.'s; Jack Morehead, Yosemite N.P.; Robert Benton, Crater Lake N.P.; Neal Guse, Mount Rainier N.P.; and, Robert Chandler, Olympic N.P.

Introduction

Text Information

General

Someone once said, "Believe half of what you read . . ." Although the editors have made every effort to impart a considerably higher percentage of accuracy to the information which follows, the spirit of this proverbial dictum should pervade the use of this guidebook. Having a disability may make the visitor more vulnerable to the consequences of misinformation than would be the case with the non-disabled traveler; more care is therefore warranted. Park visitors with a disability must use this book not as the final step in their research and planning of a park visit, but as a good first step—a first step that leads to questions and follow-up at the level of the local park. If this book accompanies the visitor to the park, it should not be used as the exclusive source of accessibility information but as a basis of further inquiry to confirm, clarify and particularize each situation. Changes occur and mistakes get made; there is no substitute for vigilance. Through correspondence, telephone calls and on-the-spot interrogation of National Park Service personnel, visitors must judge their own personal abilities in relation to each feature and offering of an individual park. **The publisher and the authors disclaim completely any liability resulting from the use of any information contained in this publication.**

The idea of making critical comparisons among the parks included in this atlas/guide was resisted for a number of reasons. Foremost was the concern that by attempting to rate one park as more accessible than another the authors would be assuming a responsibility that is best left to the individual visitor. An evaluation would have required either a good deal of subjective judgement or a rather elaborate, objective "scoring" system that in the end may not have been meaningful at all. The parks themselves differ in size, degree of cultural development (number of buildings, trails and other amenities) as well as the number of program offerings. Each reader and would-be visitor will have different accessibility requirements and different personal interests. As a result, the accessibility of the parks tend to defy direct comparisons. We have therefore left it to the reader, according to their interests and tastes, to draw their own conclusions.

Research Methods

Before embarking on an exposition of the important categories of information incorporated in the text, a background in the method of the research and its research tools will aid the user in its interpretation.

The bulk of the access information was obtained by questionnaires submitted to the selected parks, and private concessionaires serving these parks.

In devising questionnaires, the authors balanced the requirement to produce useful, accurate information, with the need to limit the size of the questionnaires. A limitation on the size was necessary in order to make a response both inviting and feasible. Park staff are extremely busy and are currently operating under mandated budget cuts. Private concessions might perceive little immediate payback for investing time in responding. In the end, seven individualized questionnaires were designed and utilized. These questionnaires combined both standardized and open-ended questioning techniques. The questions were based in large part on accessibility standards known as UFAS, the Uniform Federal Accessibility Standards mandated by The Architectural Barriers Act of 1968, as amended. (A book detailing the Uniform Federal Accessibility Standards is available at a nominal charge from: Superintendent of Documents, U.S. Government Printing Office, Washington,

D.C. 20402.) For private concessions, the access standards of the American National Standards Institute (ANSI) were applied. Additional questions were added to ascertain certain features of program accessibility, and for areas not covered by UFAS, for example, "trails" and "campgrounds," accepted standards were applied analogously.

Three types of questionnaires were sent to the parks. The questions related specifically to 1) Programming (80 questions), 2) Visitor Centers (66 questions), and 3) Campgrounds (47 questions). In the cases of both visitor centers and campgrounds, multiple copies were furnished, one for each campground and visitor center. In all cases an effort was made to direct the questionnaires to those in-park National Park Service personnel who were most responsible for coordinating and promulgating "accessibility" for visitors with disabilities. The overall response rate from the parks was outstanding.

Questionnaires were also sent to private concessions. These concessions served the selected parks, and all were members of the Conference of National Park Concessions. Four types of questionnaires were employed, one for each type of concession: 1) Food and/or Lodging (164 questions), 2) Transportation (30 questions), 3) Mercantile (63 questions), and 4) Outdoor Experience/Adventure (15 questions). Where it was appropriate, multiple copies were furnished. In general, information for non-respondents is not included.

Access Rating

Based on questionnaire responses, the various park features, buildings, programs and private concessions were evaluated in relation to their accessibility. For general purposes, "access" refers the access requirements of a wheelchair user. The nature of "access" as it refers to other visitors—those with visual, hearing or developmental disabilities—is indicated by specific description. For example, the statement that "The XYZ Film at the Visitor Center is accessible" refers only to access by wheelchair users. If there are additional access features of this program, such as film captioning or printed script, they are described specifically. Since the vast majority of access descriptions relate to the needs of visitors with mobility impairments, access information for visitors with visual, hearing or developmental disabilities has been highlighted by symbols in the margins to make them easier to identify.

"Accessible" or "fully accessible" means that a particular feature meets all or nearly all of the applicable access requirements as provided by the Uniform Federal Accessibility Standards. "Reported to be accessible" is a slightly downgraded version of "fully accessible." This rating was applied when information was furnished that indicated a feature was accessible, but that full, explanatory details were not provided on the questionnaire.

"Accessible with assistance" or "usable" applies to features which fail to meet one or more of the UFAS criteria but may still offer the potential for access by individuals who either have the help of a second party or might have the ability to use their wheelchair in an above-average or athletic manner. A smooth pathway with a steep gradient; a rough or sandy travel surface; a door requiring excessive force to open; a small, unbeveled change of level—all these might successfully be negotiated either with some assistance or exceptional skill, and therefore would have been given this classification. A flight of stairs would not.

"Not accessible" or "inaccessible" applies to features which, when they are judged against UFAS, may have multiple failings or a single, radical failure to meet standards. Some examples would include an access route to a visitor center which includes stairs, or a restroom with a door too narrow to admit a wheelchair user. Features and places rated "not accessible" may still be accessible to visitors with less severe mobility impairments, e.g., someone using a walker may be able to negotiate a set of stairs. Visitors with disabilities that are unrelated to mobility likely are capable of entering such facilities (with or without assistance) and must look to the text for particulars addressing their specific needs.

In most cases the text will contain detailed information describing any deviation from UFAS and will provide other relevant particulars.

Park Contact Office

The first information furnished concerning a park is the address and telephone number of that office within the park which is most directly responsible for addressing the needs of visitors with disabilities. In some cases this is the office of the Park Superintendent. In many cases, however, it is the "Accessibility Coordinator," "Special Populations Coordinator," "Public Information Officer" or similar office that is most prepared to provide the kinds of specialized information required.

Communication with this office should be a first priority in planning a visit, both to confirm and update the information found in this book and to pursue specific interests and needs. The parks are in continuous change, and given the current interest and momentum in "access," there is a good chance that additional accessibility will be available at the time of contact.

Depending on staff and available skills, some parks have the potential to pre-arrange special programming for visitors with disabilities. Where they occur, such possibilities are noted in the text. The office listed under this heading would be the most appropriate contact to initiate any of these arrangements.

Winter Visitation

This text section notes any factors that affect a winter visit. Some park facilities may be closed during the winter season; in others special considerations may apply.

Safety

This text section addresses personal safety considerations. If the subject matter were given an all-inclusive coverage, this short paragraph of text might have rambled for a score or more of pages for each park. As it stands, it simply highlights a few considerations deemed uniquely noteworthy for a particular park.

Elevation

A general statement concerning elevation of park roads is given in view of the fact that, because of its inverse relationship with available atmospheric oxygen, elevation has direct effects on physical stamina and cardiopulmonary function. (The atlas's park maps contain additional information on road elevations; the reader is directed to the map section under Elevation.)

Medical and Support Services

In-park clinics, if present, and the nearest hospitals are listed under this heading. Additional information is found in the Support Services maps. The nearest complete range of services is also noted. "Complete range of services" should be understood to mean the availability of: a licensed hospital, dialysis center (serving transients), retail wheelchair sales/repair, professional prosthetic and orthotic services, retail outlets for therapeutic oxygen and veterinarian services (for animal guides). Many communities may have one or more of these services available and be geographically closer to the park than those locations with a "complete range of services." See Support Services maps.

Publications

In this section National Park Service publications which have been produced *specifically* to inform visitors with disabilities are listed, along with information on how and where they may be obtained. If a park newspaper, or other publication written for general readership, contains specific access information, it is also noted.

Transportation

Some parks restrict the use of private vehicles within the park. Other parks maintain shuttle services for visitors, or license private concessions to offer transportation services. This section contains a general assessment of transportation within a park.

TDD

A statement on the availability of TDD communication for visitors with hearing disability is provided for each park.

Sign Language Interpreter

Some parks may have on staff personnel which are trained in American Sign Language (ASL), programs conducted in ASL, or emergency procedures for contacting a sign language interpreter. The availability of these services (at present they are rare) is noted in this section.

Dog Guides

Park policy concerning the use of dog guides, as well as any special consideration, is stated here.

Programs

This section is divided into organized programs and self-guided programs and it highlights their accessibility. Organized programs generally consist of films, campfire programs, ranger-led activities and scheduled events. Self-guided programs include such considerations as personal sightseeing, traveling on trails which are interpreted by signs or a printed brochure, picnicking, visiting museum displays and other types of activities in which the participant directs his or her schedule and course. Emphatically it is the visitor with mobility impairment who is addressed in this section. This is a direct reflection of the current nature of "access" at the parks; for although our questions attempted to achieve a more balanced picture, the responses emphasized access as it relates to visitors with mobility impairments.

Unless otherwise stated, "access" refers to access by a wheelchair user. Other types of access—taped or printed scripts, captioned films, tactile exhibits, program formats featuring simple pictures and explanations (for visitors with developmental disability), etc.—are stated specifically. To help the user identify programs with features of particular relevance to visitors with visual, hearing or developmental disability, margin keys will assist in locating appropriate information.

Visual Disability

Hearing Disability

Developmental Disability

Visitors with mobility-related disabilities will claim the greatest interest in the balance of the text, though the locations of general programs and available facilities would be of interest to all readers. Park locations set in **bold text** are represented on Park Maps or Insets.

Self-Guided Trails and Trails

Although in some cases the differences between self-guided trails and just "trails" are somewhat blurred, these sections contain information on all park trails that have been designed specifically for visitors with disabilities, trails that might be negotiated with assistance and, in rare cases, trails that coincidentally meet accessibility standards on grades, width and type of surface. Self-guided trails feature interpretive signs or are accompanied by a descriptive brochure; trails do not.

Exhibits

Highlighted in this section is accessibility to displays and exhibits maintained by the National Park Service or by cooperative agencies such as local historical and natural history associations.

Visitor Centers

Physical accessibility to the parks' visitor centers is described with respect to parking, path of travel to entrances, and interior facilities. The elements of the interior of visitor centers which were reviewed include the information counter, restroom, water fountain and public telephone service. The fact that this section is addressed *de facto* almost exclusively to wheelchair users, or visitors who are otherwise mobility impaired, reflects the existing situation. Aside from some occasional modifications to public telephones, physical modifications that consider visitors with hearing, visual or other disabilities are rare.

Campgrounds

Parks may designate and reserve a number of campsites for optional use by visitors with mobility impairments. Some of these sites have been designed specifically for wheelchair users and contain a number of modifications. Other designated sites simply represent camping locations which, when reviewed against all other available locations, offer the most potential for visitors using wheelchairs ("best" gradient, type of surface, proximity to restroom facilities, etc.) Park campgrounds included in this section are described in terms of their parking, paths of travel to campsite and other facilities, restrooms, sources of water, cooking grates and other modifications.

Basic Facilities Chart

For reader convenience a chart summarizing a park's accessible restrooms, water fountains and telephones has been provided. (Access to wheelchair users only is considered.) Although this chart provides a quick overview of a park, the reader must refer to the details of the text in order to develop an accurate picture of the access features and requirements of a given location.

Supplementary Information

The focus of this section is the private concessions that serve the parks. Unless otherwise stated, information regarding the concessions was obtained from our own questionnaires. Several types of concessions are considered: lodging, food service, transportation, gift shops and other retail stores (groceries, camping supplies) and "adventure experiences."

Brief statements regarding accessibility of some concessions have been taken from published sources, notably the Second Edition of "National Parks Visitor Facilities and Services," published by the Conference of National Park Concessions. In the case of these concessions, the standards applied in assessing their accessibility are unknown to the editors. The reader, who should be routinely prudent in relying on any access information, should make detailed inquiries to these concessions about all aspects of accessibility.

Concessions offering "adventure experiences," such as whitewater rafting, horseback riding and mountain climbing, were asked different questions than the other concessions. The main difference was that the standardized questions about physical access were omitted. This was done under the assumption that the physical plant where the concession operates is inconsequential to the activity, also that the activity itself is inherently not "accessible." In these cases emphasis was given to the concessionaire's experience with and willingness to serve clients with disabilities.

Reading and Using the Maps

General Features

Recognizing that a certain percentage of the readers of this guide series would have less-than-optimum eyesight, the authors have put some effort into producing maps that could be easily read. This requirement was tempered only by the desire to avoid producing graphics that would appear grotesque or cartoon-like to the general readership. Although there is a body of research on the production of tactile maps for readers with profound visual impairment, there has been very little research on mapping for readers with partial vision. As a result, the cartographic design proceeded more by intuition than on a solid groundwork of successfully proven models. Its aim was to create maps that would be readable by a "visually mixed" audience.

"Accessibility" to the parks is described in part by a series of maps which highlight the information found in the park texts. (For a description of the criteria of accessibility, see the Access Information section.) Each series is executed at an increasingly larger scale, giving a progressively "closer look" at the pertinent information. Unless otherwise noted, as in the case of the visitor center diagrams, all the maps have a standard orientation, with North at the top.

Throughout this series of maps a continuity in color theme has been applied:

The color "BLUE" is associated with accessible features. Although the Uniform Federal Accessibility Standards (UFAS) were used as the general yardstick in evaluating access, a "blue" rating is not necessarily synonymous with a feature's meeting these standards. For example, in the case of the support services surrounding a park there was no evaluation of access whatsoever. (See below under Support Services.) In some cases, such as campgrounds, there are no legally applicable Uniform Federal Accessibility Standards. The editors were compelled to interpret individual situations creatively. There are other occurrences where access to a particular feature may have required a "judgment call." These judgments, however, were made discernedly and applied conservatively.

The color "RED" is associated with features which while failing to meet Uniform Federal Accessibility Standards, may be accessible with assistance, "usable," or otherwise offer some potential for access. In addition, there are a number of park features "reported to be accessible" but the specific details necessary to confirm their accessibility had not been supplied. These features have also been indicated in red.

The color "BLACK" is associated with features that are not accessible. (Black is also used for the labeling involved in general geographic orientation: names of places, mountains, rivers, boundaries, etc.)

Locator Maps

These maps are intended to provide an orientation to a park's location and include a generalized road network of the region. Park visitors should refer to standard road maps and atlases for their basic highway navigation.

Medical and Support Services Maps

The first class of maps to contain substantive access information is "Medical and Support Services." These maps portray a selection of important products and/or services that are available within approximately a 100-mile radius of each park. Sources for this information included the local "yellow pages," the rosters of professional organizations and a computer-generated printout based on a product's or a service's Standard Industrial Code and the geographically relevant zip codes. The types of products and services included are hospitals ("H"), retail outlets selling or repairing wheelchairs ("W"), retail outlets selling therapeutic oxygen ("O"), prosthetic and orthotic products and services

("P"), dialysis centers ("D") and veterinarians, for the clinical treatment of animal guides, ("V"). Pharmacies were not included because their occurrence is so common that there seemed little need to document them; also their omission produces less cluttered maps.

In some cities and larger towns, all six of these services are available, in which case the name of the locale itself is represented in blue, e.g. "MIDDLETOWN."

Symbols for all the services are represented in "BLUE." In regard to services, the focus is on their "availability" and not their "accessibility." In other words, access to the hospitals and to the stores selling or repairing wheelchairs, or orthotics, or therapeutic oxygen, etc. is not addressed, but given the nature of some of these specialties one would hope for reasonable accessibility to them.

For detailed information concerning the services indicated, the reader should inquire at the local level. A summary of the type of dialysis and related service offered by the various centers listed on the map is available from "The List," c/o Dialysis and Transplantation, 7628 Densmore Ave., Van Nuys, California 91406, telephone: (818) 782-7328. Information concerning the selected prosthetic and orthotic services can be obtained by writing or calling the American Orthotic and Prosthetic Association, 717 Pendleton Street, Alexandria, Virginia 22314, telephone: (703) 836-7116. Other services may be contacted by referring to the local yellow pages of the phone book of the city or town named on the map. (A local library may have a surprisingly large holding of phone books from around the country.)

Park Maps

In all cases it is recommended that the visitor obtain and use the official National Park Service map of the park they are visiting. These maps, which usually accompany admission to the park or which may be obtained by mail, will furnish more complete, more detailed travel and geographic information than the maps in this guide. By using the official park map in conjunction with the maps and information in this guide, the visitor will enhance the utility of both sources of information.

The park maps which follow focus on and highlight accessibility information using the blue-red-black color theme. Features included on the map are:

Visitor Centers (labeled by name)   ABC Visitor Center

Restroom Facilities R

Drinking Water

Telephone

Medical Clinics

Amphitheaters

Campgrounds (labeled by name)   XYZ Campground

Picnic Areas

Scenic Vistas V

Self-Guiding Trails S

Trails

Where available a selection of private concessions is also represented (labeled by name), along with the facilities from the above list.

Elevation

As elevation increases, the amount of oxygen in the air decreases. This depletion has significant effects on a person's cardiovascular system; the heart and lungs must work harder to maintain the same level of oxygen, and muscles are more susceptible to exhaustion. These effects are quite noticeable, even to non-disabled people. For a person who expends considerable energy using a wheelchair or other ambulatory assists, and for those with cardiopulmonary health problems, these effects may be exaggerated. If there is any cause for concern for health risks, the prospective park visitor should consult a physician before venturing into the situation.

Persons with obstructive lung disease are particularly susceptible to the effects of elevation.

A statement regarding road elevations is positioned at the bottom of each park map. (The park text may also contain elevation information.) Changes in elevation, at 4000-foot intervals, are shown along park roads by means of orange chevrons. The chevrons always point *uphill*. The number of chevron bars indicates the level of elevation: one, above 4000 feet; two, above 8000 feet; three, above 12,000. (See map legend.)

Visitor Center Diagrams

Where available, schematic drawings of particular visitor centers have been included. The majority of these are based on architectural drawings and blueprints obtained from the National Park Service's Technical Information Center in Denver, Colorado. Some diagrams were based on blueprints or other drawings gleaned from the individual park's holdings. Others were based on hand-drawn sketches by knowledgeable park personnel. Still others represent a combination of a blueprint drawing supplemented by hand-drawn sketches with the addition of relevant outlying information not shown on the original blueprint. For this reason no map scale is provided with these diagrams. For travel distances the reader should refer to the text descriptions.

The reader should also note that the orientation of a Visitor Center Diagram may vary from the conventional, "North-at-the-top," standard. What has persuaded this deviation from the convention was the preference given to placing the main entrance "facing" the reader. Although for some diagrams, the cartographic liberties taken with the diagram orientations may require momentary patience on the part of the reader, all the diagrams contain sufficient information for successful orientation.

The blue-red-black color theme, as related to accessibility, is continued in this diagram series. As with the other maps, certain background information is presented in black. Such information may include building outlines, sidewalk locations, labeled features (e.g. "Main Entrance") and other orientational information. In such cases, the color is irrelevant to "access." If in doubt, the reader should refer to the text for clarification.

Crater Lake

**Crater Lake National Park
P.O.Box 7
Crater Lake, OR 97604
Tel. (503) 594-2211**

A half-million years ago magma from the earth's interior spewed upward, building the cone of Mt. Mazama. It was to become one of the great volcanic peaks of the Cascade Range. Throughout time many lesser magma vents developed on the slopes of the mountain. Around 4860 B.C. a massive eruption occurred, blowing so much material out of all the vents that the mountain could no longer support its own weight and collapsed. Earth and volcanic ash from this eruption lie scattered over eight states and three Canadian provinces. It is estimated that the force of the explosion was more than 40 times greater than that of Mt. St. Helens in 1980. The giant hole, or caldera, that remained was nearly six miles across. After the floor of the caldera cooled and was sealed by renewed volcanism, it began to fill with water. The volcano has not been active for at least a thousand years, allowing rain and snow to collect and fill what has become the deepest lake in the United States and the seventh deepest in the world. Crater Lake is 1932 feet deep.

Native Americans lived in the Mt. Mazama region more than 6000 years ago. They viewed its numerous eruptions, before the collapse, as a war between the gods Llao and Skell. Archaeologists suggest that humans may have witnessed the cataclysmic event. In historic time shamans, or medicine men, forbade most Indians to view the lake. No information was offered to pioneers who crossed the region for 50 years without coming upon it. It was not until 1853 that the first Europeans, a small band of prospectors, accidentally came upon the lake. Nearly fifty years later, in 1902, a National Park was established around Crater Lake.

The scenic wonder of Crater Lake is surrounded by the magnificent peaks and forests of the Cascade Range. The lake, noted for its remarkable blueness, usually remains ice-free all winter. Many species have adapted to the forest environment. Mountain hemlock, subalpine and Shasta red fir thrive even under the heavy winter snow cover. Common park animals include jays, nutcrackers, deer and squirrels. Elk, bear, fox and pine marten are present but seldom seen.

Boat tours are offered from July through early September. Rim Drive, a 33-mile road encircling the lake, has many scenic turnouts. Information is available

Climate Chart

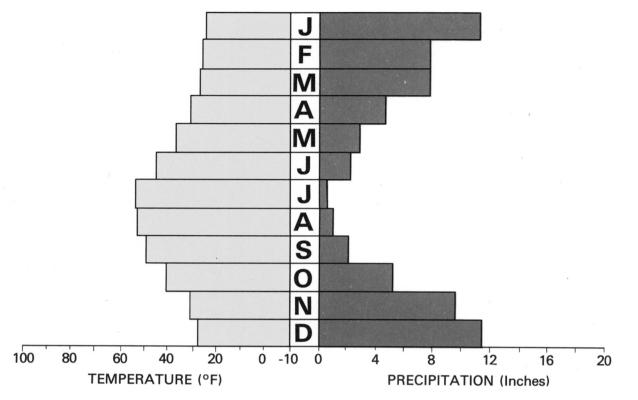

TEMPERATURE (°F)   PRECIPITATION (Inches)

Station Location: Park Headquarters
Station Elevation: 6475 feet

at the visitor center in Rim Village and at the Steel Center (open all year), located near park headquarters three miles south of Rim Village.

General Information

Weather

Average monthly temperatures during the summer hover around 60°F. The summer season is also the driest. Winter is the wettest season with most of the precipitation falling in the form of snow. Snowfall totals average 45 feet per year. The maximum snow depth recorded at Rim Village is 21 feet. Average monthly temperatures for the winter season range in the mid-20s.

Winter Visitation

The park is open during winter. Visitors should be prepared for heavy snow (40 to 50 feet annually) and icy roads. Few facilities remain open.

Safety

Bears are seldom seen but they sometimes visit the campgrounds. Read park literature about bears and take proper precautions.

Elevation

Park elevation ranges from 4405 feet at the south entrance to 8926 feet at Mount Scott. Hillman Peak reaches 8156 feet and is the highest point of Rim Drive. The elevation of Rim Village is 7100 feet. Thin air at these high elevations can make physical activity difficult even for healthy persons. Visitors with heart or respiratory problems may wish to consult their physician.

Medical and Support Services

The nearest hospitals are located in Klamath Falls, Medford, Central Point and Ashland, Oregon, all south of the park. The nearest complete range of ser-

Medical and Support Services

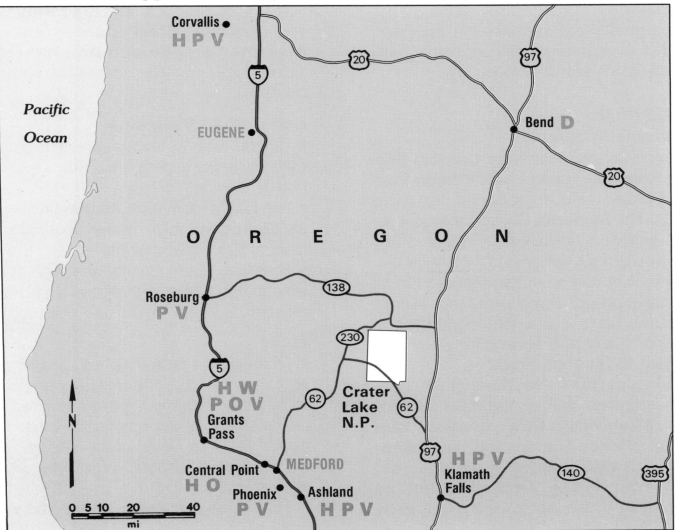

vices can be found in Medford and Eugene, northwest of the park.

Publications

• There are no publications available that directly address the needs of visitors with disabilities.

• Information in brochures about the physical requirements and other aspects of specific park resources is available in a limited sense. Such information is not always listed specifically for visitors with disabilities and may be contained along with general park information. For example, the Visitor Services section of "Crater Lake Reflections" features an abbreviated inventory of "accessible features" under the heading "Disabled Visitors". "Reflections" is available at the Main Entrance, visitor centers, information stations and concessions.

Transportation

Private cars may be used for travel in the park. Alternate means of transportation include a tour boat on the Lake (visitors must be ambulatory) and the Rim Van (12 passengers, no modifications for wheelchair users). Private vehicles and buses may travel the same route as the van.

Sign Language Interpreter

There are currently no park personnel with signing skills on staff. There are no pre-arrangements to contact an interpreter in the event of an emergency.

TDD

There is no TDD capability within the park.

Dog Guides

Dog guides are permitted in the park. Caution is recommended as some trails may be too steep for dogs.

Programs

Organized Programs

• Programs given at **Rim Center, William Steel Center** and **Rim Village Visitor Center** are all reported to meet UFAS. The **Mazama Campground Amphitheater** may not meet UFAS, but may be usable by visitors in wheelchairs. Wheelchairs can be accommodated in all seating areas for these programs. These locations have accessible parking and paths of travel and restrooms which are reported to be accessible.

• Park personnel use descriptive, concrete language during narratives at **Sinnott Memorial, Rim Center, Rim Village Visitor Center** and the **Campground Amphitheater.** Park personnel sometimes include items that can be touched at those locations as well as at the **William Steel Center**.

• Printed scripts of some verbal interpretations are available at the **William Steel** and **Rim Village Visitor Centers**.

• The **Rim Village Visitor Center** has excellent displays, including many examples of park wildlife (preserved birds, animals and geological specimens.) Tactile maps and other informational materials (books, posters, pictures for sale) are also available.

• When necessary, park personnel utilize simple photographs, pictorial illustration or other means to assist visitors with developmental disabilities in their appreciation of park features. Simple oral presentations and basic reasoning techniques are used. Special arrangements for such presentations are possible. There are no programs specifically designed to address the needs of visitors with developmental disabilities.

• A-V programs are held in at **Rim Center, William Steel Center** and the **Mazama Campground Amphitheater**. These locations are accessible with assistance.

Self-Guided Programs

• There are no accessible self-guiding trails available in the park. (See *Trails* section.)

• The park's main features can be seen by car from overlooks. Many overlooks are reported to be accessible.

• There are many picnic areas with accessible picnic tables and accessible portable toilets.

Trails

• There are no park trails accessible to visitors using wheelchairs. However, some trails have extended grades that do not exceed 1:20, or have grades less than 1:12 punctuated by level areas which may have potential for access for some visitors with mobility impairment.

• The Crater Rim walk is reported to be fairly level.

Exhibits

• General information about the park environment that is well-illustrated by photographs and other pictorial means is available in the many visual exhibits in the park. Exhibits in the Visitor Centers include some with adequate clearance for approach and viewing by wheelchair users.

• Adequate, even lighting, high contrast photography and non-glare glass have been used in exhibit design. Interpretive labels have been designed for maximum contrast.

• Tactile exhibits are located at **Sinnott Memorial, Rim Village Visitor Center** and **William Steel Center**.

• Interpretive signs are neither routed nor raised.

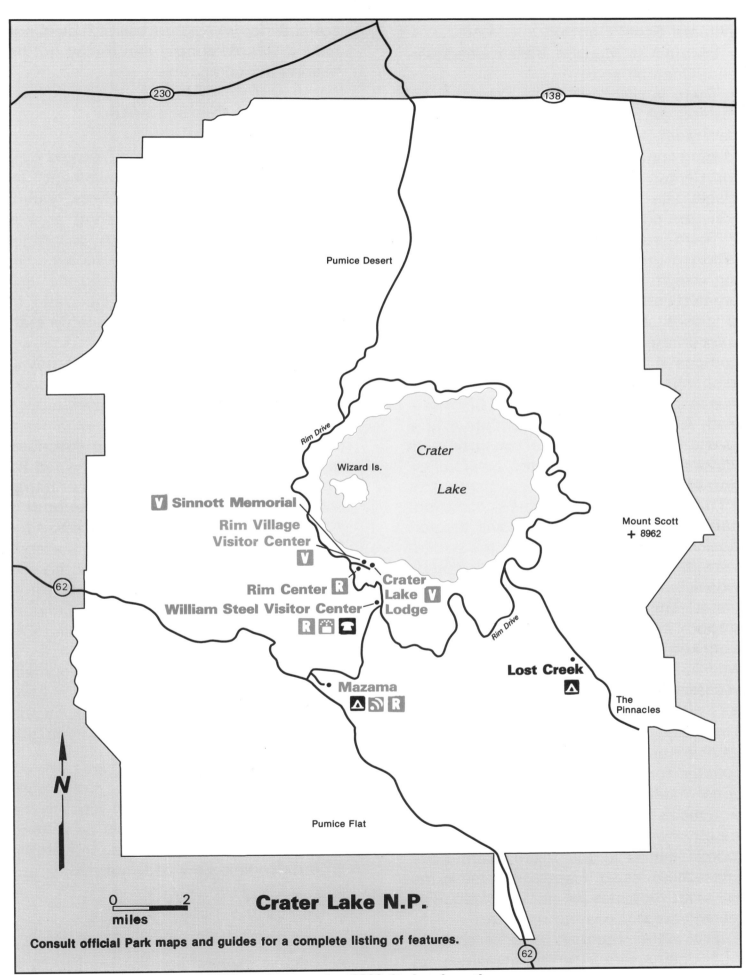

230

138

Pumice Desert

Rim Drive

Crater

Wizard Is.

Lake

Mount Scott
+ 8962

V **Sinnott Memorial**

**Rim Village
Visitor Center**
V

Rim Center R

Crater
Lake V
Lodge

William Steel Visitor Center
R 🏠 ☎

Rim Drive

Lost Creek
⛺

The
Pinnacles

62

• **Mazama**
⛺ 🏕 R

N

Pumice Flat

0 —— 2
miles

Crater Lake N.P.

Consult official Park maps and guides for a complete listing of features.

62

Park roads range from 4400 to just under 8000 ft. in elevation.

Visitor Centers

William Steel Center

• Located at Munson Valley Headquarters. Open all year.

• There is reserved, accessible parking, marked with a symbol painted on the pavement, and an accessible passenger loading zone about 125 feet from the Visitor Center. Necessary curb cuts are in place. The parking area and the loading zone are paved, level and smooth.

• There is a continuous route of travel, reported to be accessible, from the parking area to the building. In summer there are two entrances, but the main entrance is closed during the winter. Both entrances are accessible. The pathway is composed of asphalt and flagstones. Level changes in the flagstone path which are less than one-half inch have not been beveled. A ramp with a rise less than 1:12 is in use on this route. It is equipped with handrails, edging and an all-weather, non-slip surface.

• The Visitor Center contains information, natural history exhibits, a movie theater, book sales, and restrooms. In the auditorium there is space to accommodate wheelchair users in the seating arrangement. The floor of the auditorium is smooth carpet (no pile). The main exit from the auditorium is not accessible to wheelchair users; two alternate exits are accessible.

• The information desk is positioned at an accessible height for wheelchair users but there is not adequate clearance under the counter for a front approach. Informational material is either placed within a 24-inch reach or staff assistance is available.

• Both the men's and the women's restroom facilities in the Visitor Center are fully accessible. Hot water is in use at the sinks but the pipes are not insulated. The faucets are not easy to operate.

• The water fountain is accessible to wheelchair users. The spout allows for use of a cup and the lever moves easily.

• The public telephone is not positioned correctly for wheelchair users. It does not have a volume control and it may not be hearing-aid compatible.

Rim Village Visitor Center

• Open in summer only.

• There is reserved parking, marked by a symbol painted on the pavement; its width is less than UFAS. Necessary curb cuts are in place. The parking area is paved, level and smooth. A passenger loading zone is present. The distance between the reserved parking and the Visitor Center is 50 feet, but the route of travel to the accessible entrance (in rear) requires additional travel.

• There is a continuous route of travel, reported to be accessible, from the parking area to the building's rear entrance on the lake side. The pathway is at least three feet wide with a surface described as "a little rough". It is unobstructed by abrupt level changes. A cement ramp with a rise less than 1:12 is in use on this route. It is equipped with handrails, edging and an all-weather, non-slip surface.

• The information desk is higher than 34 inches and lacks knee clearance for a frontal approach. Pamphlets, brochures and other material are placed within a 24-inch reach.

• There are no restrooms, water fountain or phone located inside this Visitor Center. Usable restrooms are located in the parking lot serving the cafeteria/gift shop.

Sinnott Memorial

• The Sinnott Memorial is adjacent to the Visitor Center. It is accessible by a steep ramp; assistance is required. It features an outstanding view of Crater Lake.

Rim Center

• Located at Rim Village. Open in summer only.

• There is reserved parking, marked by a symbol painted on the pavement. Parking

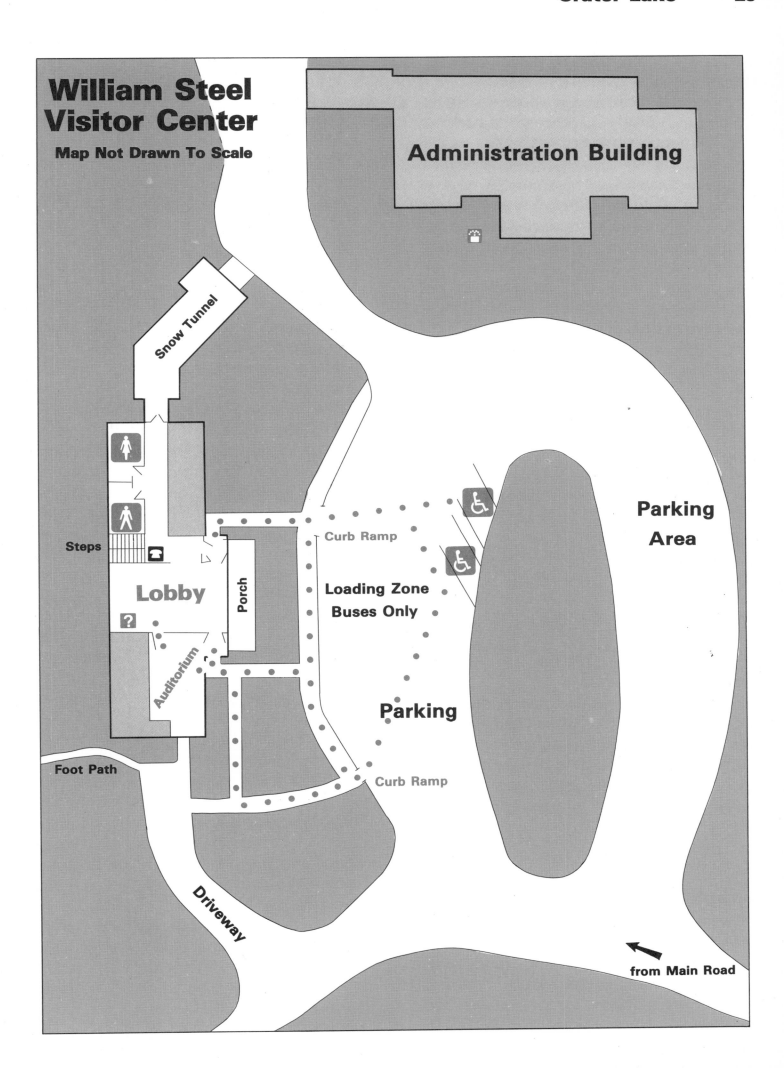

William Steel Visitor Center

Map Not Drawn To Scale

Administration Building

Snow Tunnel

Steps

Lobby

Porch

Auditorium

Foot Path

Driveway

Curb Ramp

Loading Zone Buses Only

Parking

Curb Ramp

Parking Area

from Main Road

spaces are not extra-wide but the parking area has a smooth, level, paved surface. Necessary curb cuts are in place.

• There is a continuous route of travel which runs steeply uphill from the parking area 50 feet to the entrance. Assistance is required. The route is three feet wide and is asphalt paved.

• The porch leading into the auditorium where audio-visual presentations are conducted has no ramp. Visitors are required to negotiate one 12-inch step. The interior has movable seating (folding chairs) to accommodate wheelchair users. The walls feature many visual displays: logging equipment, snow equipment, artifacts and taxidermy of indigenous wildlife.

• There are no restrooms located in the Center. Usable restrooms are located in the main parking lot. A curb cut is present. The door pull is very heavy. There is adequate turning space inside; the stall space is adequate but no grab bars are in place. Only cold water is in use. A soap dispenser is properly positioned but both the paper towels and mirrors are too high.

• No water fountain or telephone were reported.

Campground
Mazama Campground

Mazama Campground campsites are not accessible to wheelchair users. Twenty cabin units are scheduled to be completed as of the date of this publication. Two of these cabin units will be designated for use by visitors with disabilities.

Supplementary Information

• **Canteen of Oregon** and **Crater Lake Lodge, Inc.** (Crater Lake, OR 97604) operates a number of lodging, food, gift, and service concessions. *Note: The following information was obtained independently of the concession, by ques-tionnaires filled out by a local disability advocate.*

A fast-food cafeteria and gift shop concession is located in its own building. The cafeteria, upstairs lounge and bar are open during the summer season only. There are two reserved parking spaces for visitors with disabilities. They are marked by a symbol painted on the pavement which cannot be seen when there is snow cover. The width of the spaces (10 feet and 9.5 feet) does not meet UFAS. The parking area is level, smooth and paved. The distance from parking to the winter/summer entrance is 50 feet; to the main entrance, 250 feet. The main entrance is not accessible to wheelchair users.

The best route of travel to the concession's facilities is over asphalt, then tight-weave carpet. The route of travel has un-beveled changes in level between one-quarter and one-half inch. A 6-foot wide, walled ramp is in use at the winter/summer entrance. Its grade exceeds 1:12. Assistance may be required. The ramp has handrails and an all-weather, non-slip surface. The winter/summer entrance has a 26-inch wide door. The door pull is easy but the there is no space between the door and the graded ramp. No landing is present at the bottom. The door cannot be opened to exit by a wheelchair user without assistance.

Once inside, the route of travel to the restroom is accessible but the restroom itself is not. The entrance is less than 32 inches wide and involves a difficult sharp turn. The room has inadequate turning space and the stall is less than 36 inches wide. Grab bars are improperly positioned and flimsy.

The gift shop features some aisles too narrow to negotiate using a wheelchair and much of the merchandise is out of reach; assistance by staff is available. Most service counters are higher than 34 inches.

USGS – J.P. FRIEDMAN

The cafeteria is reached through the gift shop. The self-serve counter is too high (beverages, etc., out of reach); silverware, trays, cups, etc. are out of reach. There is movable seating which can accommodate wheelchair users. The lounge and bar upstairs are not accessible to wheelchair users.

• **Crater Lake Lodge** (usually open June through September) offers food and lodging to visitors. Because of space limitations, reservations are recommended for both food and lodging (early spring is best). Staff is reported to be helpful and friendly but has had no special training or sensitization to the needs of guests with disabilities.

There is signed, reserved, accessible parking on a smooth, level, paved surface. Parking is located about 50 feet from the concession. A passenger loading zone which does not meet UFAS is located about 20 feet from the concession. The route of travel to the concession entrance has a blacktop or concrete surface and is at least 36 inches wide; overall it is smooth and level although sections of it need re-surfacing. A temporary ramp, accessing the sidewalk, is located adjacent to the two reserved parking spaces. The ramp is constructed of three-quarter-inch plywood with a surface of rubber belting; it has a one-inch lip. Assistance may be required. The main entrance has a flight of steps. The·only usable entrance is located on the south side of the building. As one travels from the reserved parking spaces, this alternate entrance is reached before the main entrance. There is a two-inch lip at the doorway so assistance may be required.

Assistance in entering the facility by concession staff is not readily available. Guests may pre-register if registration at desk is physically difficult. Registration is done by card; a clipboard is available for use. Assistance in filling out the registration card or in orienting guests to the layout and emergency procedures of the lodge is available from the staff. The route of travel from registration to the rooms does not meet standards and will require assistance. The route is of adequate width and its surface is a tight-weave carpet on which maneuvering is easy. Along the route a 6-foot permanent ramp with a grade in excess of 1:12 must be negotiated. The ramp has walls and a non-slip surface. The upper floors are not accessible to wheelchair users.

There are no specially modified rooms available. In typical rooms the doorways are 28 inches wide. Furniture elements are placed too close to each other for easy movement by a wheelchair user. Door locks are well-positioned and easy to use with one hand or without being able to be seen. The light switch is within reach of a wheelchair user (inside door, right hand) and an additional lamp is controlled within reach of the bed. The mattress top is at an appropriate height and the bed is on casters. There are no phones in the guest rooms. Multi-sensory emergency alarms are not in use. There is no braille information.

Bathroom doors are 22 inches wide and swing inward. There is not adequate space for turning inside bathroom. No properly positioned grab bars are in use. The toilet seat is positioned between 17 and 19 inches from floor. Sink is low enough to be operated by wheelchair users but lacks adequate clearance underneath; hot water pipes are not insulated. Some rooms have a shower stall but stalls have inadequate dimensions and lack grab bars or other modifications to make

them usable.

Communal restrooms are located in the hallway between the registration desk and the halls to rooms. Communal restrooms do not meet standards. The doorways are 32 inches wide but the toilet stalls are only 22 inches wide. The stall doors swing outward. Stalls lack grab bars. The toilet seats are at appropriate heights. Sinks are low enough but lack adequate clearance underneath; hot water pipes are not insulated. There are no shower facilities in the communal restrooms.

The public telephone in the lodge lobby is out of reach. The drinking fountain is accessible.

Parking for dining facilities is identical to those for the lodge. Access to dining facilities is at the south end of the building and involves negotiating a two-inch threshold. Assistance may be required. The travel route is through hallways to the rooms (see above). Food is served at ta- The travel route is through hallways to the rooms (see above). Food is served at tables. Seating is flexible and staff will rearrange tables and chairs to accommodate guests. Tables are at an appropriate cilities in the dining room. (See description of communal restroom facilities above.)

Additional comments: Dining room and lodge sitting room (with fireplace) have impressive vistas with ample viewing space and good windows. Exit doors to the viewpoint have a one-inch threshold (for snow). The viewpoint surface is concrete; protective fencing is in place.

Basic Facilities

	Restroom	Water Fountain	Telephone
Mazama Campground	●		
Rim Center	●		
William Steel Visitor Center	●	●	●

Lassen Volcanic

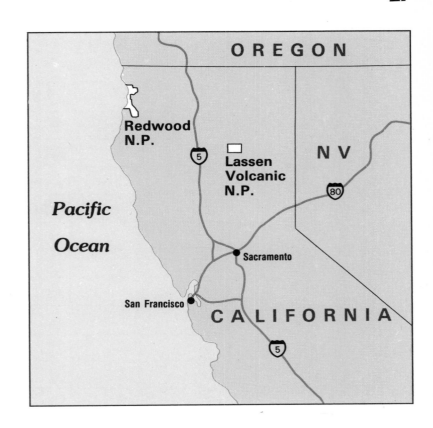

Superintendent
Lassen Volcanic National Park
P.O. Box 100
Mineral, CA 96063
Tel. (916) 595-4444

At the southern tip of the Cascade Mountains is a 106,000-acre expanse of conifer forests, mountains and wilderness lakes. This area, dominated by Lassen Peak (10,457 feet), has been designated as Lassen Volcanic National Park. Lassen Peak, a plug-dome volcano, has been calm for a long period with intermittent eruptions last occurring from 1914 to 1921. Other volcanic features found here are hot springs, steaming fumaroles, sulfurous vents and the beautifully symmetrical cinder cone.

The woodlands of the park are composed of a variety of pines, firs and cedars, as well as broad-leaved trees such as aspens and cottonwoods. Willows and alders border many of Lassen's streams and lakes. Wildflowers are usually abundant from mid-June through September.

Lassen Park receives ample precipitation throughout the year, creating a variety of habitats rich in animal life. More than 50 kinds of mammals, 150 species of birds, 12 different types of reptiles and amphibians and an abundance of insects are found here.

Lassen Park Road winds around three sides of Lassen Peak and affords many beautiful views of the volcano. Along the route visitors will find examples of destructive volcanic action as well as vistas of woodlands, lakes and rushing brooks. The park is open all year, but the trans-park road is closed by heavy snow from the end of October until early June.

General Information
Weather

Summers here are warm, with average monthly temperatures ranging in the 60's°F. Summer is the driest season. July is the driest month, receiving less than one inch of rainfall. Winters are cold with heavy snowfalls.

Winter Visitation

The park is open during winter. A first aid room is located at the Ski Chalet.

Safety

Stay on established trails at all times. In areas with hot springs or steam, keep small children under strict physical control to avoid burns or accidents. Ground crusts which appear safe may be dangerously thin.

Climate Chart

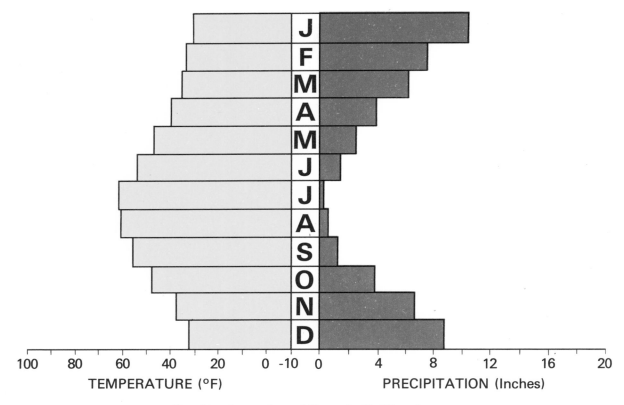

Station Location: Mineral, California
Station Elevation: 4911 feet

Elevation

Elevations on main roads range from 5800 to 8500 feet. The average elevation of main park features is 7000 feet. The thin air can be dangerous for visitors with respiratory ailments or heart disease. Overexertion should be guarded against.

Medical and Support Services

The nearest complete range of services can be found in Redding, California, west of the park. The nearest hospitals are located in Redding and Red Bluff, west of the park and Chester and Susanville, east of the park.

Publications

• Brochures are available that provide descriptions of the physical requirements and other aspects of specific park resources.

• The park newspaper, "Lassen Park Guide" includes program schedules and other information.
• An audio cassette tape tour of the park is available.

Transportation

Private cars may be used for travel in the park.

Sign Language Interpreter

• There are currently no park personnel with signing skills on staff. Arrangements are in place to contact an interpreter in the event of an emergency.

TDD

There are no TDD capabilities in the park.

Dog Guides

Dog guides are permitted in the park.

Medical and Support Services

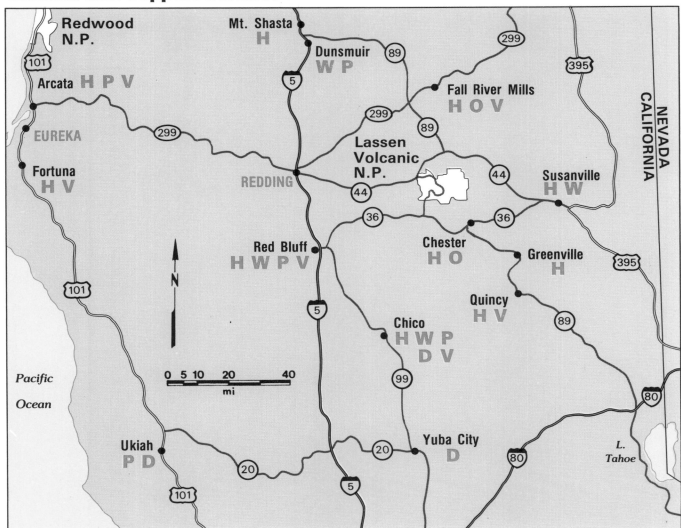

Programs

Organized Programs

Many programs about the natural and cultural history of the park are offered throughout the season. Visitors should obtain the calendar of scheduled naturalist activities. The July-August schedule is printed in the summer edition of the park newspaper "Lassen Park Guide". June and September schedules differ.

There are visual presentations (displays) at all park contact stations.

Park personnel use descriptive, concrete language in all program narratives. Touchable items are included in the programs conducted at **Manzanita Lake Visitor Center**. Simple photographs, pictorial illustrations or other means are used to assist visitors with developmental disabilities appreciate park features during the Volcanic Products Program, Pioneer Demonstration and Indian Demonstration. Simple verbal presentations and basic reasoning techniques are utilized during programs.

• Programs held at **Manzanita Lake Amphitheater** and **Manzanita Lake Visitor Center** are accessible. There is an accessible parking area and an accessible path of travel from the parking area to the Amphitheater via a spur road that accommodates vehicles. Allowances have been made for wheelchairs in the program seating area at the Amphitheater. There are reported to be accessible restrooms here.

• Verbal interpretation of programs at Indian Ways Nature Trail, cinder Cone, **Lassen Peak** and **Bumpass Hell** are available in printed form.

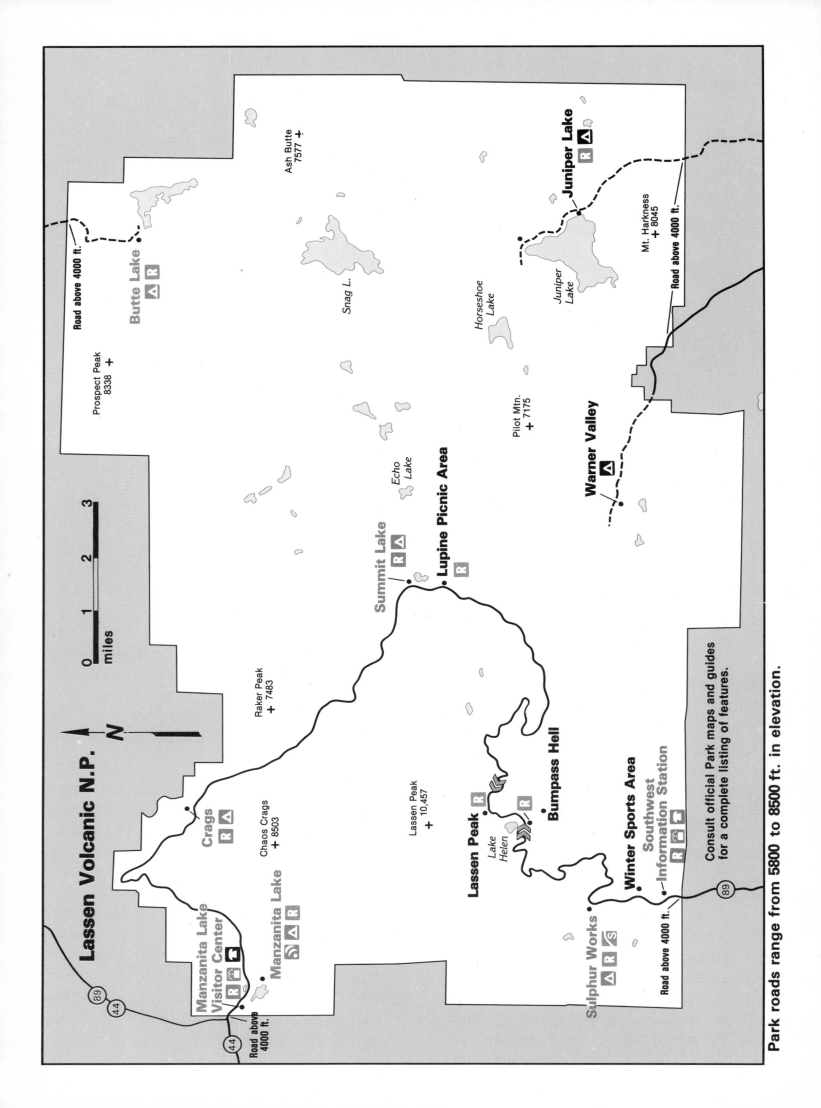

Lassen Volcanic N.P.

N

miles
0 1 2 3

Manzanita Lake Visitor Center R 🅿️ 🏠

Manzanita Lake 🛶 Ⓐ R

Road above 4000 ft.

Crags R 🏠

Chaos Crags + 8503

Raker Peak + 7483

Lassen Peak + 10,457

Lassen Peak R

Lake Helen

Bumpass Hell

Winter Sports Area

Southwest Information Station R 🏠 🏠

Sulphur Works Ⓐ R 🅂

Road above 4000 ft.

Summit Lake R Ⓐ

Echo Lake

Lupine Picnic Area R

Prospect Peak 8338 +

Ash Butte 7577 +

Butte Lake Ⓐ R

Road above 4000 ft.

Snag L.

Juniper Lake R Ⓐ

Horseshoe Lake

Juniper Lake

Mt. Harkness + 8045

Road above 4000 ft.

Pilot Mtn. + 7175

Warner Valley Ⓐ

89

44

89

44

Road above 4000 ft.

Consult official Park maps and guides for a complete listing of features.

Park roads range from 5800 to 8500 ft. in elevation.

• Programs held at the **Southwest Contact Station** are accessible. There is an accessible parking area.

• A-V programs are shown at **Manzanita Lake Amphitheater** which is accessible (see above).

Self-Guided Programs

• There are no self-guiding trails specifically designed for visitors with mobility impairments.

• A portion of **Sulphur Works** Trail is reported to be accessible (see *Trails*, below). There is accessible parking. At Sulphur Works there is an accessible path of travel from the parking area to the Thermal Feature Area.

• A cassette tour has been developed for visitors with visual impairments and is available at either entrance station. The taped program uses highly descriptive language. The cassette program is also available in printed form.

Trails

• A portion of the **Sulphur Works** Trail is accessible to wheelchair users with assistance. Part of the trail is paved and there is also a boardwalk section with railings. This trail has grades in excess of 1:12. There is accessible parking. There are reported to be accessible restrooms and water at Southwest Chalet.

Exhibits

• Book sale exhibits are reported to be accessible.

• Well-illustrated general information about the park environment is available.

• Vertical exhibits may be approached and viewed from a wheelchair with a maximum and minimum reading height of 65 inches and 54 inches, respectively, at **Sulphur Works**, Devastation Area and **Manzanita Lake Visitor Center**. Horizontal exhibits at Manzanita Lake Visitor Center have a bottom surface with a minimum of 27 inches from ground level to allow a frontal approach by wheelchair users. The horizontal top surfaces are designed to be viewed from an average eye level height of 48 inches. Objects to be handled are placed on a work surface 28 to 34 inches from ground level and within a 24-inch reach.

• Adequate, even lighting, high-contrast photographs and non-glare glass have been incorporated into exhibit design.

• Interpretive labels have been designed for maximum contrast.

• A tactile exhibit is located at **Manzanita Lake Visitor Center**.

• Interpretive signs may be routed or raised.

• Exhibits and displays make use of simple photographs, pictorial illustrations and other means to assist visitors with developmental disabilities appreciate park features.

Visitor Centers

Manzanita Lake Visitor Center

• Open early June to late September.

• There is reserved, signed accessible parking and an accessible passenger loading zone about 15 feet from the Visitor Center. Accessible curb cuts are in place. The parking area and loading zone are paved, level and smooth.

• There is a continuous, accessible route from the reserved parking to the main entrance of the Visitor Center. The pathway is paved, level and smooth. Level changes less than one-half inch have been beveled. A ramp with less than 1:12 grade is in use on this route. It is equipped with handrails, edging, and an all-weather, non-slip surface.

• The information desk is higher than 34 inches.

• The restrooms at Manzanita Lake Visitor Center are fully accessible for wheelchair users.

• The water fountain is accessible. The spout allows for use of a cup, and the lever moves easily.

• The public telephone is on an accessible

route, but it is positioned too high for wheelchair users. It does not have a volume control and it is not hearing-aid compatible.

Southwest Information Center
• Open early June to late September.
• There is reserved, signed accessible parking approximately 50 feet from the information center. There is an accessible passenger loading zone immediately adjacent to the information center. Both the parking area and the loading zone are paved, level and smooth. Accessible curb cuts are in place.
• Park information is provided at this booth. A ramp is in use. Its rise is less than 1:12 and it has handrails and an all-weather, non-slip surface. Restrooms and telephone are located nearby in the Lassen Ski Chalet.
• The information desk is accessible. Informational materials are placed within a 24-inch reach on the desk.
• Restrooms are located in the Chalet next to the information center. They are fully accessible to wheelchair users. Faucets are easy to turn and the soap dispenser has been lowered.
• The water fountain is accessible. The spout allows for use of a cup, and the lever moves easily.
• There is an accessible public telephone at the Chalet. It does not have a volume control and may not be hearing-aid compatible.

Campgrounds

Manzanita Lake Campground
• There is designated reserved parking approximately 15 feet from the campsites. The parking surfaces are level asphalt. There are accessible asphalt and gravel routes from the parking areas to the campsites.
• One restroom is fully accessible. The others are reported to be accessible but not all features have been adapted to

meet standards.
• The source of water is reported to be accessible. It is a faucet operated by knobs. There may not be adjacent clear space to allow a wheelchair user to approach.
• Cooking grills are reported to be fully accessible.

Crags Campground
• There is designated reserved parking approximately 25 feet from the campsites. The parking surface is level asphalt and gravel. There are accessible asphalt and gravel routes from the parking areas to the campsites.
• The restrooms are vault toilets which are reported to be accessible.
• The water source is reported to be fully accessible. It is a faucet operated by knobs.
• The cooking grills are reported to be fully accessible.

Summit Lake Campground
• There is designated reserved parking approximately 25 feet from the campsites. The parking surfaces are level asphalt and gravel. There are accessible asphalt and gravel routes from the parking areas to the campsites.
• The restrooms at the North end of the lake are reported to be accessible. There are vault toilets at the South end of the lake.
• The water source is reported to be accessible. It is a faucet operated by knobs.
• The cooking grills are reported to be fully accessible.

Butte Lake Campground
• There is designated reserved parking approximately 25 feet from the campsites. The parking surfaces are level asphalt and gravel. There are accessible asphalt and gravel routes from the parking areas to the campsites.
• Restrooms are accessible. In the men's room, urinals may be too high for use by visitors in wheelchairs.
• The water source is reported to be fully

accessible. It is a faucet operated by knobs.

• The cooking grills are reported to be fully accessible.

South Entrance/Sulphur Works Campground

• There is designated reserved parking approximately 25 feet from the campsites. The parking surfaces are level asphalt and gravel. There are accessible asphalt and gravel routes from the parking areas to the campsites.

• The restrooms are accessible, except that urinals may be too high for wheelchair users. Faucet fittings have been adapted for use by visitors with disabilities.

• The water source is reported to be fully accessible. It is a faucet operated by knobs.

• The cooking grills are reported to be fully accessible.

Warner Valley Campground

• There are no campsites which are specially designed for visitors with disabilities, though one is being developed.

• The restrooms are not located on an accessible route but the facilities are vault toilets which meet UFAS.

• The water source is not located on an accessible route but the source itself meets standards. It is a faucet operated by knobs.

• The cooking grills are accessible.

Juniper Lake Campground

There are no campsites specially designed or especially appropriate for visitors with disabilities. The restrooms are vault toilets which are accessible.

Basic Facilities

	Restroom	Water Fountain	Telephone
Bumpass Hell	●		
Butte Lake Campground	●		
Crags Campground	●		
Juniper Lake Campground	●		
Lassen Peak	●		
Lupine Picnic Area	●		
Manzanita Lake Campground	●		
Manzanita Lake Visitor Center	●	●	●
Southwest Contact Station	●	●	●
Sulphur Works Campground	●		
Summit Lake Campground	●		
Warner Valley Campground	●		

Big trees are a notable feature of the western parks.

NPS — M.W. WILLIAMS

Mount Rainier

**Superintendent
Mount Rainier National Park
Ashford, WA 98304
Tel. (206) 569-2211**

For those driving toward the Park, the hours that follow the first glimpse of the mountain seem an eternity as the peak appears and then disappears behind successively closer ranges. When the lower peaks are finally left behind, Mount Rainier looms directly ahead, standing almost 8000 feet higher than the surrounding landscape.

At 14,410 feet, Mount Rainier soars into the upper atmosphere and acts as a barrier to moisture-laden air flowing eastward from the Pacific Ocean. The result is the creation of spectacular cloud formations as well as the production of large amounts of snowfall. Snowfall is heaviest from Paradise Ranger Station up to 9500 feet. Above this elevation the mountain rises above the wet Pacific air masses and snowfall decreases.

Mount Rainier's presence may be so overwhelming that little attention is paid to the encircling forests. These are old-growth forests of the Pacific Northwest with Douglas fir, red cedar and western hemlock towering more than 200 feet above the fern-draped valley floors. Beginning in April at the lowest elevations

and ending at the tree line in August or early September, wildflower displays and vibrant, greening meadows follow the melting snow.

Wildlife is easy to spot on the open sub-alpine landscape. Deer and mountain goats may be seen in the distance, but marmots seem to be of the most interest to the majority of visitors. The most popular sub-alpine section of the park is the Paradise area. On the northeast flank of Rainier, the Sunrise area offers the most sweeping road vistas of the mountain and the string of volcanic peaks along the Cascade Range.

Mount Rainier's glacial system is the largest single mountain system in the continental United States. There are 25 named glaciers on the mountain. On warm days the glaciers provide constant reminders of their continued activity in the form of avalanches of ice, snow and rocks. At any time a huge mass of snow and ice may break loose, making the mountain extremely dangerous.

Mount Rainier is considered to be a dormant volcano, but geologists are unable to assure that it will not reawaken at

Climate Chart

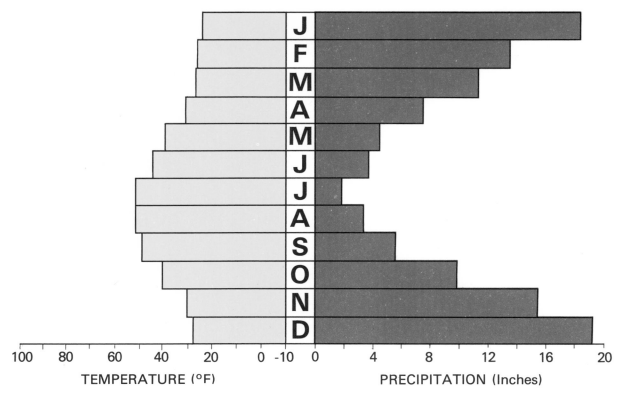

Station Location: Paradise Ranger Station
Station Elevation: 5427 feet

General Information

Weather

Average monthly summer temperatures range in the 50's °F. The summer season is the driest, with July receiving less than two inches of rainfall on the average. Winter monthly temperatures average in the 20's but precipitation may be heavy, with December and January receiving the most snowfall.

Winter Visitation

The park is open during winter. Visitors should be prepared for deep snow and cold, wet weather. Snow closes roads for some time in the future. Mount Rainier National Park continues to be an active landscape of swirling clouds, roaring rivers, luxuriant growth and rugged mountains.

short periods. Chains may be required for winter driving. Except for the roads from Nisqually Entrance to Paradise, all other park roads are usually closed from late November to June or July.

Safety

In the back country be prepared for sudden and extreme weather changes. Be alert for bears. Sliding on snowbanks may result in injury. Snowbanks sometimes hide rocks, cliffs, or even streams. In the springtime, snow bridges over streams may collapse under a person's weight. Stay off glaciers. They contain deep, hidden crevasses. Rocks fall continuously from their snouts. Stay away from the ends of glaciers.

Elevation

Roads range from 2000 to 6400 feet in elevation. When over 4000 feet, visitors should caution against overexertion.

Medical and Support Services

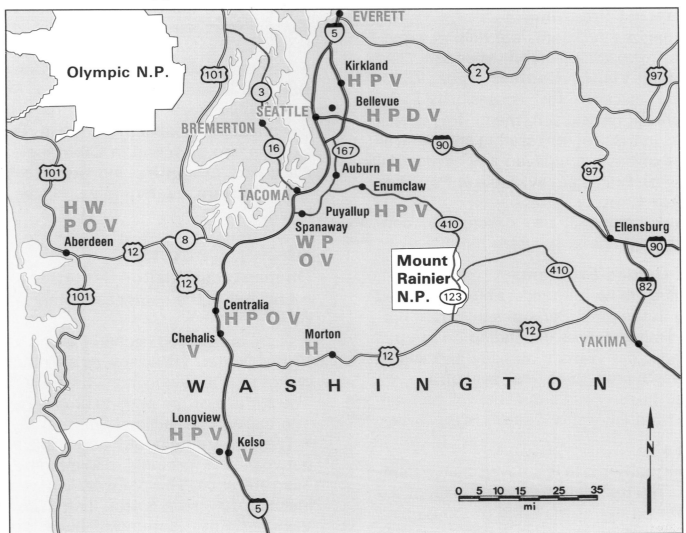

Medical and Support Services

Emergency help and first aid are available at any ranger station. The nearest hospitals are located in Morton, Washington, 30 miles south, Puyallup, 60 miles northwest, and Enumclaw, 40 miles north. The nearest complete range of services can be found in Tacoma, west of the park, and in Yakima, east of the park.

Publications

• There are no publications available that directly address the needs of visitors with disabilities.
• Information in brochures about physical requirements and other aspects of specific park resources is very general.
• General information about the park environment is available that is well illustrated by photographs or other pictorial means.

Transportation

Private cars may be used for travel in the park. Public transportation to the park is available from Seattle during the summer months.

Sign Language Interpreter

There are no interpreters with signing skills on staff. Arrangements have been made to contact an interpreter in case of emergency.

TDD

There is no TDD capability within the park.

Dog Guides

Dog guides are permitted in park. Contact the park staff for suggestions about trail use.

Programs

Organized Programs

• Organized programs are held at **Long-mire, Paradise, Ohanapecosh** and **Sunrise Visitor Centers**. (See *Visitor Center* section for accessibility.) Allowances have been made for wheelchairs in the program seating areas and all paths of travel are paved and accessible.

• A-V programs are available at **Paradise Visitor Center**.

• Park personnel use descriptive, concrete language in program narratives.

Self-Guided Programs

• There are no fully accessible self-guided trails in the park. Parts of some trails provide limited access depending on the trail surface, the visitor's mobility and available assistance. (See *Trail* section.)

• Self-guiding audio material will be available from the Visitor Centers in the future.

Trails

• **Nisqually Vista** is a paved trail at Paradise. The trail starts 100 yards west of the Visitor Center at the edge of the parking area, however the start is not accessible to wheelchair users. The trail may be reached by another trail that connects from the Visitor Center. The Nisqually Vista Trail is steep in places (grades over 1:12) and assistance may be needed. There are no sheltered rest areas or support facilities on the trail. There is no cut-off loop to shorten distance. There are no barriers to obstruct views for visitors in wheelchairs.

• Other trails include Trail of the Shadows at **Longmire**, Hot Springs Trail at **Ohanapecosh** and Emmons Trail at **Sunrise**. These trails are not fully accessible and visitors should check with a ranger to assess feasibility.

Exhibits

• Some of the older exhibits are not accessible to wheelchair users. Accessible exhibits have adjacent clear space to allow approach by wheelchairs. Some exhibits have a top surface designed to be viewed from an eye-level height of 48 inches.

• Large-print information is available at **Sunrise Visitor Center** exhibits. Some interpretive labels in the park have been designed for maximum contrast. Tactile exhibits can be found in **Ohanapecosh, Paradise, Longmire** and **Sunrise Visitor Centers**. Interpretive signs are routed.

Visitor Centers

Ohanapecosh Visitor Center

• Located in the southeast corner of the park.

• There is reserved, signed parking at the Visitor Center. These spaces are not extra wide, so assistance may be necessary. The surface of the parking area is paved. The walkway is inclined.

• There is a continuous accessible route between the reserved parking and the main entrance. This pathway is paved but inclined. Its grade is less than 1:12. The Visitor Center entrances have double doors.

• The information desk and publication sales display are accessible to wheelchair users.

• Restrooms are described as "partly accessible". Restroom doors are reported to be difficult to enter for wheelchair users. Stalls are not wide enough to permit adequate clear space for a wheelchair user to turn, but stall doors swing outward and are wide enough to allow a wheelchair through. The stalls do have properly positioned grab bars. In the men's room there is no urinal low enough for wheelchair users. Sinks are placed at an appropriate height for wheelchair users.

• The water fountain is accessible. The spout allows for use of a cup and the lever moves easily.

• The public telephone is located at the front of the Visitor Center between the

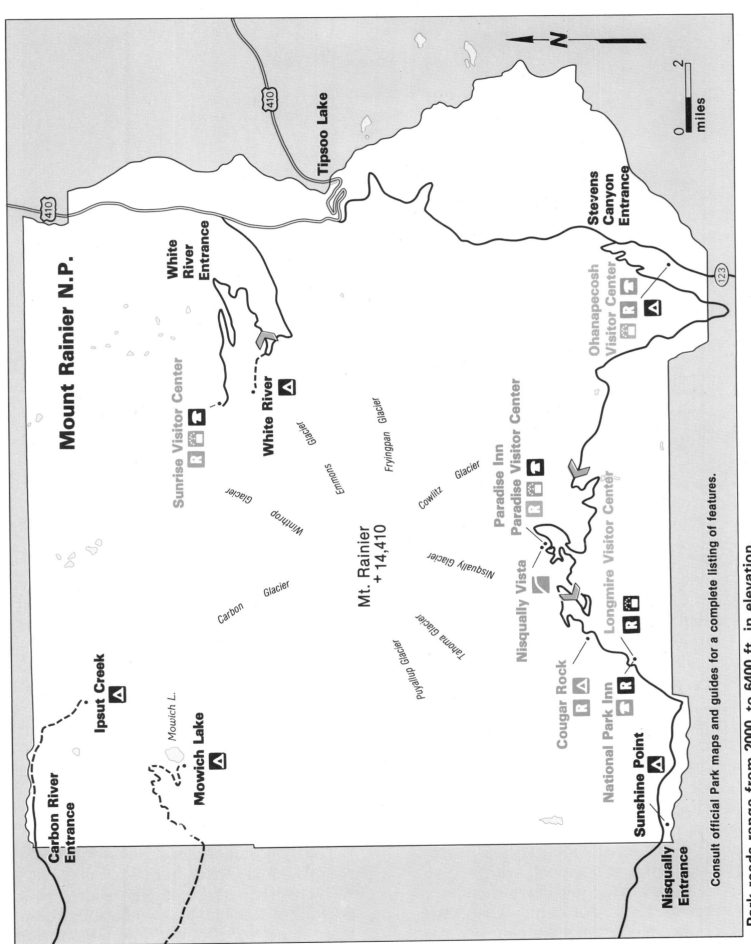

Mount Rainier N.P.

Carbon River Entrance

Ipsut Creek

Mowich L.

Mowich Lake

White River Entrance

Sunrise Visitor Center

White River

Tipsoo Lake

Glacier

Emmons Glacier

Winthrop Glacier

Carbon Glacier

Fryingpan Glacier

Mt. Rainier + 14,410

Cowlitz Glacier

Nisqually Glacier

Tahoma Glacier

Puyallup Glacier

Paradise Inn
Paradise Visitor Center

Nisqually Vista

Longmire Visitor Center

Cougar Rock

National Park Inn

Sunshine Point

Nisqually Entrance

Ohanapecosh Visitor Center

Stevens Canyon Entrance

2 miles 0

Consult official Park maps and guides for a complete listing of features.

Park roads range from 2000 to 6400 ft. in elevation.

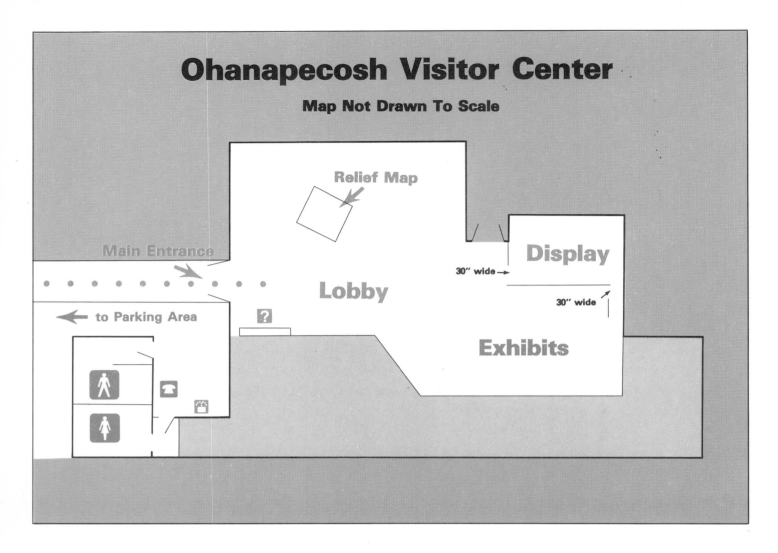

Ohanapecosh Visitor Center

Map Not Drawn To Scale

Relief Map

Main Entrance

Lobby

Display

30" wide →

30" wide →

← to Parking Area

Exhibits

restrooms. It is accessible, though the cord may be short. This telephone does not have a volume control and may not be hearing-aid compatible.

Paradise Visitor Center
• There is reserved, signed, accessible parking directly in front of the Visitor Center. The parking area is paved, level and smooth.
• There is a continuous accessible route of travel from the reserved parking to the main entrance. This pathway is smooth but not level. Level changes less than one-half inch have been beveled. A ramp is in use on this route. Its rise is greater than 1:12, so assistance may be necessary. The ramp is equipped with edging and an all-weather, non-slip surface.
• Access to this Visitor Center is reported to be good during the summer when the main entrance is in use. In winter, because of deep snow, an alternate en-

trance is used. For visitors with mobility impairment, flights of stairs make this entrance very difficult to use.
• The main entrance is on the first floor where information, food service and a gift shop are located. The auditorium and the main exhibit room are located on the second floor. The third floor contains additional exhibits. The top floor is an observation deck. These four levels are connected by means of interior ramps but their grades are greater than 1:12, so assistance may be necessary. The lowest level is reached via stairs.
• A loaner wheelchair is available on request for short-time use.
• The information desk, located on the main level, is higher than 34 inches.
• The restrooms located on the main level are fully accessible. In the men's restroom there is no urinal placed low enough for wheelchair users. One urinal is equipped with grab bars.

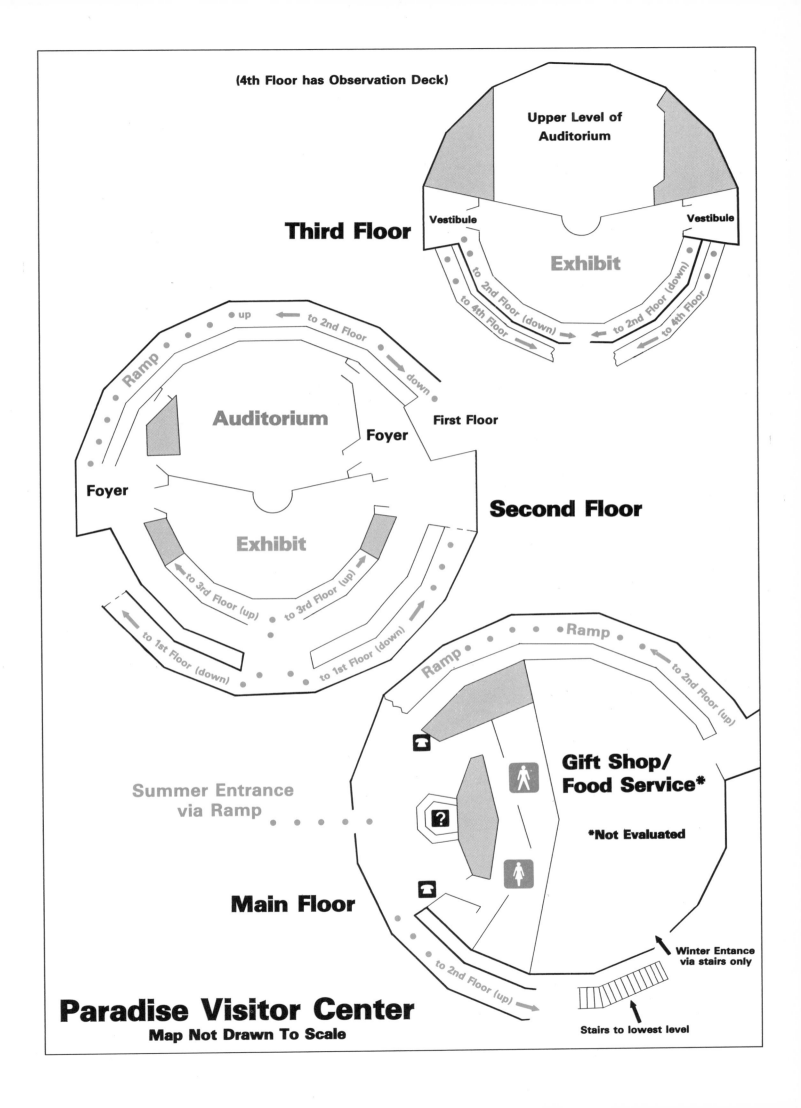

(4th Floor has Observation Deck)

Upper Level of Auditorium

Third Floor

Vestibule

Vestibule

Exhibit

to 2nd Floor (down)

to 4th Floor

to 2nd Floor (down)

to 4th Floor

Ramp

up

to 2nd Floor

down

First Floor

Auditorium

Foyer

Foyer

Exhibit

Second Floor

to 3rd Floor (up)

to 3rd Floor (up)

to 1st Floor (down)

to 1st Floor (down)

Ramp

Ramp

to 2nd Floor (up)

**Gift Shop/
Food Service***

Summer Entrance
via Ramp

*Not Evaluated

Main Floor

Winter Entance
via stairs only

to 2nd Floor (up)

Paradise Visitor Center

Map Not Drawn To Scale

Stairs to lowest level

• Additional restrooms are located on the lowest level but that floor is reached by stairs.

• The water fountain is reported to be accessible but the spout may not be placed low enough for wheelchair users. The spout allows for use of a cup, but the lever may be difficult to operate.

• The public telephone is located on an accessible route, near the information desk and restrooms on the main floor. The telephone is not positioned for wheelchair users. It does not have a volume control and it may not be compatible for use with hearing aids.

• Another telephone is located in the lower level (winter entrance) near the restrooms; its characteristics have not been evaluated.

Longmire Museum

• Located in the southwest corner of the park at Longmire, between the Ranger Station and the National Park Inn.

• There is reserved, signed, accessible parking about 50 feet from the Museum. Accessible curb cuts are in place. The parking area is paved, level and smooth.

• There is a continuous accessible route from the reserved parking to the main entrance. The pathway is paved, level and smooth. Level changes greater than one-quarter inch have been beveled.

• The information desk is higher than 34 inches.

• There are no restrooms in the Museum.

• Restrooms are located in the Longmire Plaza and in the National Park Inn. These restrooms are not accessible to wheelchair users but may be usable. In both locations neither the men's nor women's restrooms have a 36-inch wide stall and there is not enough clear space in the stalls to turn a wheelchair. In the men's restroom there is no urinal placed for wheelchair users. The sinks are not low enough for wheelchair users.

• The water fountain is located on an accessible route but it is not placed at an appropriate height for wheelchair users. The spout allows for use of a cup, but the lever may be difficult to operate.

• There is a public telephone on the porch of the National Park Inn. It is on an accessible route. The telephone is positioned properly for wheelchair users but the cord may be too short. It does not have a volume control and it may not be hearing-aid compatible.

Sunrise Visitor Center

• Located in the northeast corner of the park. Elevation: 6400 feet.

• There is reserved, signed, accessible parking. The minimum travel distance from parking to the Visitor Center is 100 yards. Accessible curb cuts are in place. The parking area is paved, level and smooth.

• There is a continuous usable route of travel from the reserved parking to a side entrance. The pathway is paved, level and smooth. Level changes less than one-half inch have been beveled. A ramp on this route has a rise greater than 1:12, so assistance may be necessary. It is equipped with edging and an all-weather, non-slip surface.

• The information desk is higher than 34 inches. However, the installation of a new, accessible desk is imminent.

• The restrooms are located in a separate building. They are reported to be accessible. There may not be a wide toilet stall with adequate turning space for a wheelchair in either the men's or women's restrooms. Properly positioned grab bars may not be in place. In the men's restroom there is no urinal placed for wheelchair users. Sinks may not be placed at an appropriate height for wheelchair users.

• The water fountain is located at the edge of the parking area. It does not meet UFAS. It is positioned low enough for wheelchair users but does not have adequate clearance underneath. The spout

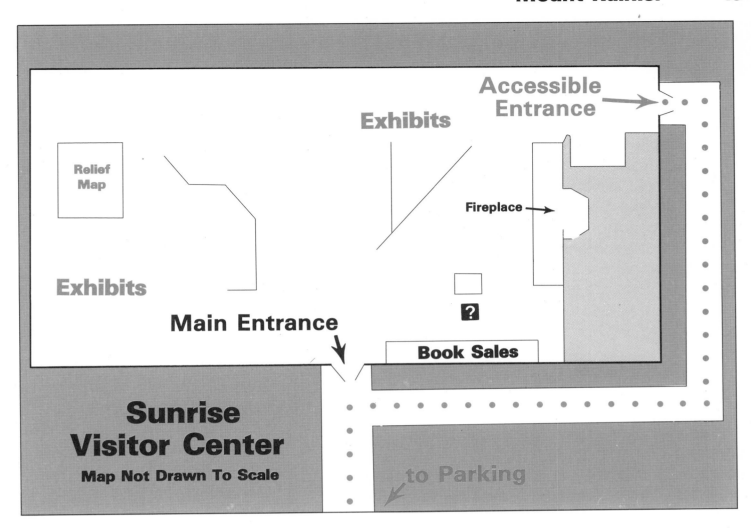

Accessible Entrance

Exhibits

Relief Map

Fireplace

Exhibits

Main Entrance

❓

Book Sales

Sunrise Visitor Center

Map Not Drawn To Scale

to Parking

may not allow for use of a cup. The operating lever moves easily.

• The telephone is located near the restrooms, between the Visitor Center and the Lodge. It is not positioned low enough for wheelchair users and does not have a volume control. It may not be hearing-aid compatible.

Campgrounds

Cougar Rock Campground

There is one campsite designated for visitors with disabilities. It is reported to be accessible. Restrooms are reported to be accessible to visitors in wheelchairs. An accessible picnic area is also reported at this location.

Other Campgrounds

Ohanapecosh, White River, Ipsut Creek, Mowich Lake, and Sunshine Point Campgrounds have no campsites which are designed specifically or especially appropriate for visitors with disabilities.

Supplementary Information

• **Mt. Rainier Guest Services** (Star Route, Ashford, WA 98304) operates lodging, food and ski touring concessions in the park.

National Park Inn offers food and lodging. The staff has not been sensitized to the needs of guests with disabilities but has had experience serving guests with mobility impairments. There is reserved, signed parking on a smooth, level, asphalt surface. Parking spaces are too narrow to meet current accessibility standards. A special parking permit is required. Curb cuts are present but may not meet standards.

A paved pathway at least three feet wide leads to the concession entrance. The entrance doorway has an unbeveled level change greater than one-quarter inch and may require assistance. A wooden ramp with a grade less than 1:12 provides access to the porch. The ramp is four feet wide, is equipped with handrails and has a 3.5-inch safety edging. If assistance is required in entering and exiting the concession, the staff will assist.

Registration is not done by card. Staff cannot offer special assistance with registering. Rooms are not accessible to wheelchair users and the path of travel does not meet standards. Most doors are 29 inches wide. Doors and locks are very difficult to use. Rooms contain no modifications or retrofittings. Most in-room bathroom doors are 28 or 29 inches wide and swing inward. Inside the bathroom there is not a five-foot clear space for maneuvering a wheelchair. Showers and other bathroom facilities are inappropriate for wheelchair users.

Public restrooms are located on the second floor and are not accessible to wheelchair users. An accessible telephone is reported to be located on the porch off the lobby.

Dining room parking and access are the same as described above for the main entrance. The dining room staff has had experience serving guests with mobility impairments (wheelchair users) and unaccompanied guests with developmental disabilities. Tables are inappropriately designed for wheelchair use. Some aisles are 36 inches wide. If needed, the staff will assist. Restrooms serving the dining facilities are not accessible to wheelchair users but may be usable. They may present difficulty to guests with other mobility impairments. (See Longmire Museum, in the *Visitor Centers* section, for a description.)

National Park Inn (museum and gift shop) sells books, maps and slides. This store has had experience serving guests with disabilities when accompanied by a caregiver or companion. There is accessible, signed and reserved parking on a smooth, level, paved surface. It is located about 50 feet from the concession. Accessible curb cuts are in place. The route

of travel to the entrance is three feet wide but the ramp has a grade in excess of 1:12, so assistance is required. The ramp is permanent and is equipped with handrails, edging and an all-weather, non-slip surface.

The store interior has an open sales area with no aisles. Shelves have a maximum height of 5.5 feet. There is an accessible route to the service counter. The store is staffed by a single employee, so significant assistance is not available to patrons with disabilities.

The Paradise Inn offers food and lodging. The staff has not been sensitized to the needs of guests with disabilities but has had experience serving guests with mobility impairments and special medical needs. There is reserved, signed parking on a asphalt surface which may not be smooth and level. Parking spaces are too narrow to meet current accessibility standards. A special parking permit is required. Curb cuts are in place but they may not meet standards.

The distance from the reserved parking to the lodge entrance is 100 feet. A passenger loading zone is located 10 feet from the entrance. The surface is concrete with exposed aggregate. Curb cuts of unknown standards are in place. Bellhops will assist a guest with disabilities when needed.

The "most accessible" entrance is by way of a route at least three feet wide over a concrete surface with exposed aggregate. This route has an unbeveled level change greater than one-quarter inch and may require assistance. Bellhops will assist. There are two additional entrances to the dining room by means of short, 42-inch ramps with grades of 1:12. Assistance may be required.

Registration is done by card. A clipboard is not available. There is a usable route of travel, at least three feet wide, connecting the registration desk and rooms. Level changes between one-quarter and one-half inch have been beveled. The route is over parquet flooring and short-pile rug. Ramps are in use on this route and ramp grades slightly exceed 1:12. Ramps lack handrails. They are 8.5 feet wide. The interior ramp has walls and the exterior ramp has edging six inches high. If necessary, the staff will assist.

The Lodge has five rooms that have been specifically modified to accommodate the needs of guests with disabilities. They are rooms numbered 310, 316, 318, 320 and 322. Reservations are recommended but not required. No specific lead time was suggested. No specific details about the modified rooms were furnished.

The following descriptions apply to the Lodge's room in general. Each room either has two beds or can have an additional bed placed in the room. The entrance door is 36 inches wide. Furniture is arranged so that there is not four feet, three inches between major furniture elements. Information about door locks, light switches and mattress height was not furnished. The bed is not attached to the floor but it cannot be raised for medical equipment. There are no modifications in the room for guests with visual or hearing disabilities. An audio-visual alarm system is not in place.

The in-room bathroom has a doorway 36 inches wide; the door swings out. The bathroom does not have an interior five-foot clear space for maneuvering a wheelchair. The bathroom is equipped with grab bars. Height of the toilet seat is 16.75 inches. Sinks are low enough for operation by wheelchair user, but frontal approach is not possible because of inadequate clearance. Hot water pipes underneath are not insulated. Showers are located in the bathroom tubs. Tub walls are 15 inches high and no grab bars were reported.

The food concession is located in the Lodge dining room. Parking and main access are the same as given above for the Lodge. There are two additional entrances to the dining room by means of short, 42-inch ramps with grades of 1:12. Assistance may be required. The serving staff has had experience serving guests with disabilities including guests with mobility impairments and developmental disabilities.

Table surfaces are 28 to 34 inches high. Floor space is appropriate but there is not enough clearance under the table for a guest to use a wheelchair while seated at the table. Aisles are not at least 36 inches wide. The dining staff will assist where necessary.

Restrooms that serve the dining area are reported to be on an accessible route. The doorways are 36 inches wide. Stalls are too narrow and lack adequate clear space to meet UFAS. Stall doors swing out. One grab bar is in place on the back wall. Sinks are reported to be usable but hot water pipes are not insulated. Faucet levers, mirrors, soap and towel dispensers and hot air hand-dryers are reported to be usable.

Additional communal restroom facilities are located in the lobby hallway area leading to the Paradise Inn Annex. Entry requires opening two doors which may be difficult for wheelchair users and may require assistance. Doorways are 36 inches wide. Modified stalls are 54 inches wide and 55 inches deep. The stall doors swing out. The toilets are positioned at an appropriate height. The men's restroom lacks a lowered urinal. Sinks are accessible but hot water pipes are not insulated. Faucets have protruding ends for grasping and work easily. Mirrors, soap and towel dispensers and hot air hand-dryers are positioned for wheelchair users.

The Ski Touring Center offers ski and snowshoe equipment rentals and instruction. The staff has had no training, sensitization or experience regarding clients with disabilities but is willing to assist. Arrangements for specialized group instruction would be possible with advance planning. "We would be pleased to work with any group willing to take the necessary preparation to permit such an undertaking."

Basic Facilities

	Restroom	Water Fountain	Telephone
Cougar Rock Campground	●		
Longmire Visitor Center	●	●	
National Park Inn	●		●
Ohanapecosh Visitor Center	●	●	●
Paradise Inn	●		
Paradise Visitor Center	●	●	●
Sunrise Visitor Center	●	●	●

Olympic

Special Populations Coordinator
Olympic National Park
3002 Mount Angeles Road
Port Angeles, WA 98362
Tel. (206) 452-4501

The Olympic Mountains are the result of the movement of two of Earth's crustal plates. Millions of years ago, the Pacific plate began to move eastward and slip under the edge of the North American continent. Sedimentary rocks and lavas were scraped off the ocean floor. Those lavas now form a horseshoe shape of basalt along the east and north portions of the Park. Over millions of years, layer upon layer of sedimentary rock were pressed against the previous layer forming a twisted folded jumble of rock.

Eventually this mass of rock became attached to the edge of the continent and rose upward, creating newly formed mountains. Immediately the erosional forces of wind, running water, glaciers, snow and varying temperatures began to wear away the ruggedness of these mountains. Valleys were cut, even newer mountains were carved and streams ran seaward carrying sediment and debris back to the ocean floor. The Olympic Mountains are young by geologic standards but the process of plate movement, uplift and erosion continue.

The mountains form a barrier to moisture-laden air sweeping eastward from across the Pacific Ocean. It reaches the coast and flows upward over the barrier. As the air rises it cools, resulting in heavy precipitation. Then, as it descends east of the mountains, the air warms and retains its moisture, bringing that area little rainfall. This effect is so extreme that the wettest spot in the continental United States (Mount Olympus receives 200 inches of precipitation per year) lies only 40 miles west of the driest coastal region north of southern California.

Today remnant glaciers wear away the high country of the Olympics. Meltwaters from these glaciers quickly turn into rushing rivers. At the tree line, forests begin to crowd the riverbanks. Soon the slopes level off, the waters slow and become warm enough to support fish. Rivers flowing toward the Pacific are the spawning grounds for steelhead and cutthroat trout and salmon. At an elevation of 1000 feet, these westward flowing rivers enter the rain forest. Finally, in less than 50 miles, the waters enter the sea.

Climate Chart

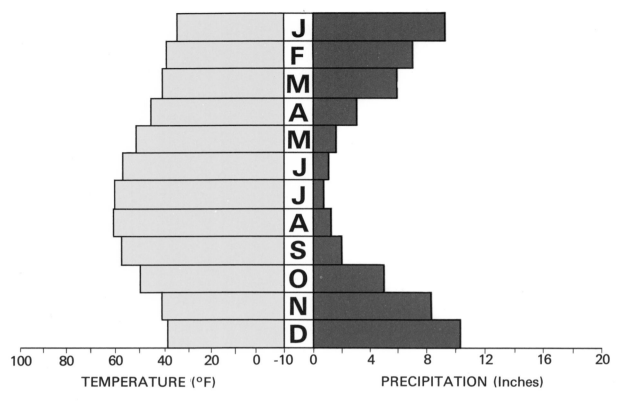

Station Location: Elwha Ranger Station
Station Elevation: 2548 feet

Olympic National Park is host to a great diversity of climate, vegetation and wildlife with seacoast, rainforest, mountain forests, fir groves, wildflower-carpeted meadowlands, sub-alpine forest and alpine tundra; Olympic contains just about every environment imaginable.

Deer, marmot, black bear, goats and Roosevelt elk all live in the Park. Along rivers, lakes and the coast live wildlife of a different sort; harbor seals, river otters, raccoons and shore birds. Even gray whales may be seen off the coast in spring and fall.

Olympic's natural beauty and diversity offer visitors an opportunity to fully experience and appreciate the relationship of people with the wild.

General Information
Weather

At any time of the year, rainfall may last for days at a time. This is particularly true from October through March when three-quarters of Olympic's precipitation occurs. Temperatures near sea level stay mild, usually reaching only the low 70's °F in summer, and remain in the 40's during the winter.

Winter Visitation

The park is open for winter visitation.

Safety

When hiking the beach, round the headlands only on an outgoing tide to avoid being trapped. The tide and cliffs permit no escape. Be prepared for sudden and extreme weather changes.

Elevation

Elevations of park roads range from 1110 feet on U.S. Route 101 to 5200 feet on Hurricane Ridge. When above 4000 feet, visitors should caution against overexertion. Elevations in the park range from sea level along the 58-mile coastal strip to the 7965-foot summit of Mt. Olympus.

Medical and Support Services

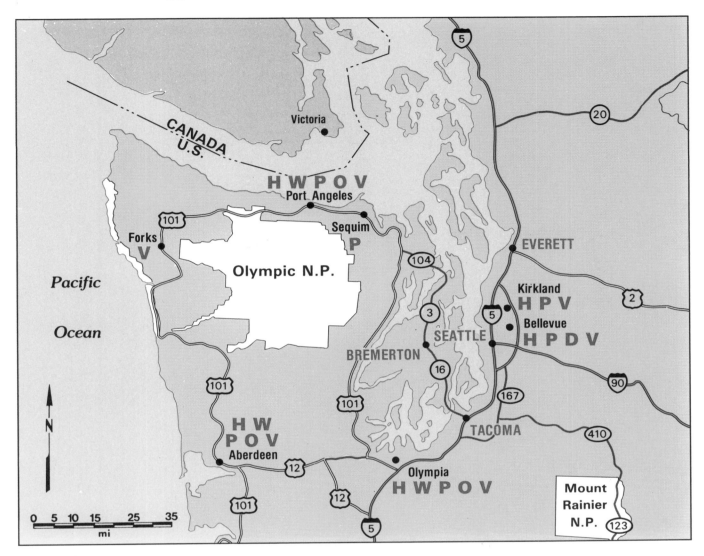

Medical and Support Services

The nearest hospitals are located in Port Angeles, Bremerton and Aberdeen. A complete range of services can be found in Bremerton and Seattle.

Publications

• Currently there are no publications available that directly address the needs of visitors with disabilities.

• Park staff and signs provide descriptions of the park that inform visitors with disabilities of the physical requirements and other aspects of specific park resources.

• The staff provides information about the availability and location of alternative interpretive devices or services for visitors with visual disabilities. A guide to Hurricane Ridge is available on cassette tape.

Transportation

Private vehicles may be used for travel in the park. Shuttle bus tours within the park are reported to have the capability of accommodating the needs of visitors with mobility impairments. Visitors should inquire at visitor centers for specific information.

Sign Language Interpreter

Currently there are no park staff trained in sign language and the park has no pre-arrangements to contact an interpreter in the event of an emergency.

TDD

TDD capability for out-going calls only is available at the Pioneer Memorial Museum.

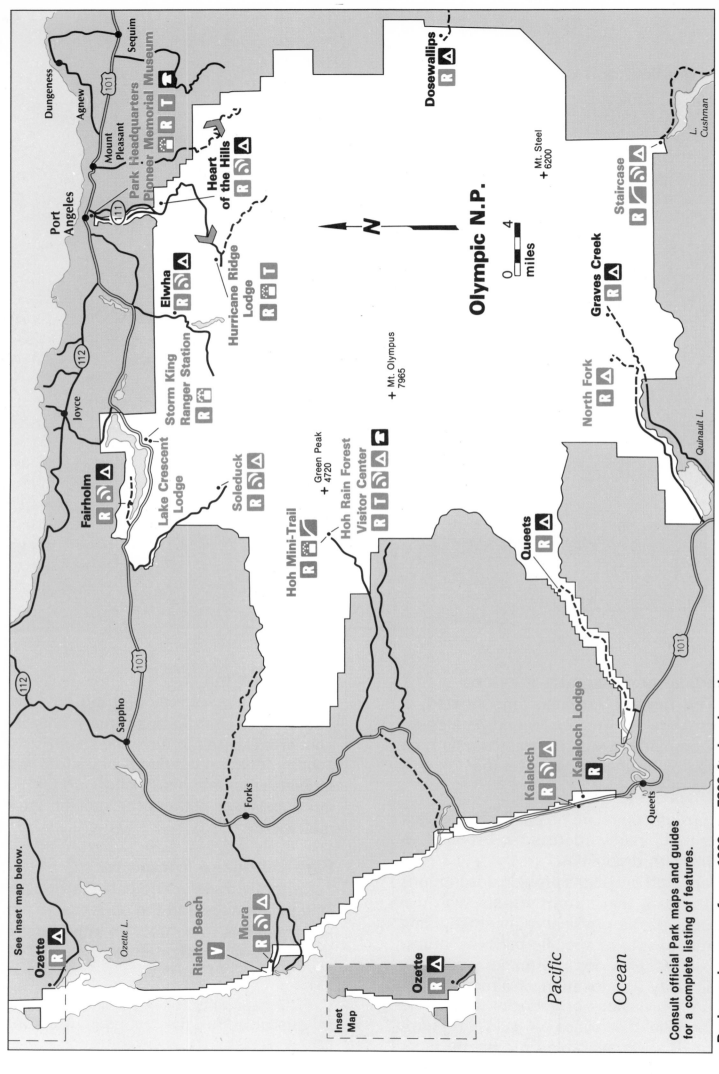

Olympic N.P.

Dungeness

Sequim

Agnew

101

Mount Pleasant

Port Angeles

Park Headquarters · Pioneer Memorial Museum

111

Heart of the Hills

Hurricane Ridge Lodge

Elwha

Storm King Ranger Station

112

Joyce

Lake Crescent Lodge

Fairholm

Soleduck

Green Peak + 4720

Hoh Mini-Trail

Hoh Rain Forest Visitor Center

Mt. Olympus 7965 +

N

Dosewallips

Mt. Steel 6200 +

L. Cushman

Staircase

Graves Creek

North Fork

Quinault L.

Queets

0 — 4
miles

Sappho

101

Forks

Ozette L.

Rialto Beach

Mora

Ozette

See inset map below.

Kalaloch

Kalaloch Lodge

101

Queets

Pacific

Ocean

Inset Map

Ozette

Consult official Park maps and guides
for a complete listing of features.

Park roads range from 1000 to 5200 ft. in elevation.

Dog Guides

Visitors may use dog guides in the routine course of visiting park features and programs.

Programs

Organized Programs

• In general, personally-led programs during the summer are conducted in locations that are accessible with assistance.

• A slide show at **Hurricane Ridge Lodge** is reported to be accessible. (See also *Visitor Center* section.)

• The "Varied Treasure" slide program conducted in the **Pioneer Memorial Museum** is reported to be accessible, although there are no special allowances made for wheelchairs in the program seating area. The program presentation utilizes highly descriptive language. The museum and picnic area may be accessible (see *Visitor Center* section).

• The **Pioneer Memorial Museum** may occasionally feature sensory exhibits which include wildlife, seashore and botanical subjects. The herbarium at the Visitor Center is reported to be accessible.

• Evening programs are offered during the summer. They are held at campground amphitheaters; comments about accessibility are listed below. The campgrounds are reported to have accessible restrooms (see *Campgrounds* section).

Elwha - Signed parking with curb cut.
Fairholm - No signed parking. Lighting on the pathway is inadequate. Assistance is required.
Heart O'The Hills - Signed parking, paved trail with adequate width and lights. Approach is steep enough to require assistance.
Hoh Rain Forest - Designated parking and paved walkway. Steep approach will require assistance. Seating area is not level.

Kalaloch - Access described as being "good".
Mora - Described as "Accessible".
Soleduck - Described as "O.K.".
Staircase - The well-lighted path has a grade which is excessively steep. Seating area is not level. Assistance required.

Self-Guided Programs

• A self-guiding cassette tape describes the **Hurricane Ridge** area and is available at the **Pioneer Memorial Museum**. This program has been tested on-site by staff and blind consultants prior to its public use.

• Lookout Point, a wayside exhibit on the **Hurricane Ridge** Road, is accessible with assistance in negotiating the 4.5-inch curb to sidewalk. Once on the sidewalk, wheelchair users can access the exhibits.

• Picnic areas reported to be accessible are located at the **Pioneer Memorial Museum, Hurricane Ridge** (Picnic Areas A and B) and **Hoh Visitor Center**. Access to these areas has not been evaluated with respect to UFAS.

• **Rialto Beach** Area has designated parking. A cedar ramp provides excellent views of the beach and surf.

• Salmon Cascades Overlook at **Soleduck** is reported to be accessible with assistance. No designated parking or curb cuts present.

• Nature trails at **Staircase** are difficult to access and would require assistance. There is no designated parking but area is flat and has no curbs or drop.

Trails

• The **Hoh Mini-Trail** in the Hoh Rain Forest is reported to be accessible without assistance and was designed for use by visitors with mobility impairments. It consists of a paved trail about a quarter-mile in length. It has extended grades that do not exceed 1:20. Rest areas feature benches with back and arm rests. The trail surface is reported to have a high visual contrast with surrounding terrain. Accessible parking, restroom facilities and water are reported.

• There are a number of other paved trails within the park. All require some assistance. These trails include: the trail that runs from **Mora** to **Rialto Beach** (0.12 miles); the **Hurricane Ridge** Big Meadow Trails (0.5 miles) and the Hurricane Hill Trail (1.5 miles). All trails are reported to have surfaces which are in high visual contrast with surrounding terrain. The Hurricane Hill Trail is open in the summer only and its first one-third mile offers the mildest gradient.

Exhibits

• In general, exhibits make use of adequate and even lighting, and interpretive labels are designed with maximum visual contrast for readability.

• The booklet, "Olympic—The Story Behind the Scenery" is well illustrated by photographs and pictorial means and may be appropriate to aid individuals with developmental disabilities interpret the park environment. It explains the natural and human history of the park.

• **Pioneer Memorial Museum** features the most accessible exhibits in the Park but some may not meet UFAS. One exhibit features objects that can be touched. The Natural History Discovery Room's exhibits include recordings of animal sounds.

• A tactile interpretation experience is possible in the **Elwha** area where there is a raised-relief map of the park on display.

Visitor Centers

Pioneer Memorial Museum and Visitor Center

• Located at Park Headquarters in Port Angeles and open all year. The following information has not been evaluated in relation to UFAS.

• There is reserved parking near the Visitor Center, but the spaces may not be extra wide. A curb cut is in place.

• There is a ramp in use to access the main entrance and the restrooms. The rear entrance is also ramped.

• Restrooms are located just outside the main entrance. The restrooms are accessible.

• The water fountain is reported to be accessible.

• The public telephone is located outside the main entrance. It is placed too high for wheelchair users.

• TDD capability for outgoing calls only is available inside the Visitor Center.

Hoh Visitor Center

• There is reserved parking near the Visitor Center. A curb ramp is in place.

• There is reported to be a continuous accessible route from the parking area to the main entrance of the ranger station.

• Restrooms in the Visitor Center are reported to be accessible. Mirrors are not low enough for wheelchair users.

• Restrooms in adjacent campground Loop A are also reported to be accessible and can be reached from the Visitor Center by a paved trail.

• The water fountain is located outside the restrooms. Its accessibility was not evaluated.

• The public telephone is too high for wheelchair users; it has a rotary dial.

Storm King Ranger Station

• Located on Barnes Point at Lake Crescent.

• There is reserved parking near the restrooms. Curb ramps are in place in front of the reserved parking.

• A ramp is in use on the pathway from the parking area to the Ranger Station. It is reported to be at least three feet wide and have a grade less than 1:12.

• Restrooms are located in a separate building near the reserved parking. They are reported to be accessible.

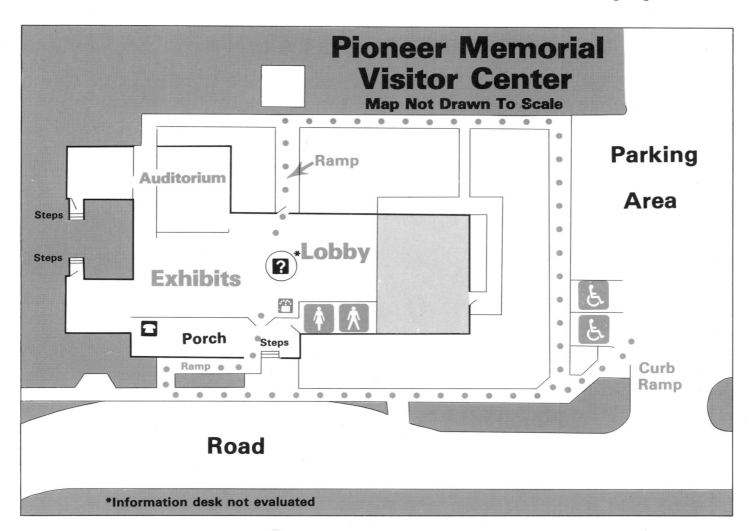

Pioneer Memorial Visitor Center
Map Not Drawn To Scale

Parking

Area

Ramp

Auditorium

Steps

Steps

*Lobby

Exhibits

Porch

Steps

Ramp

Curb Ramp

Road

*Information desk not evaluated

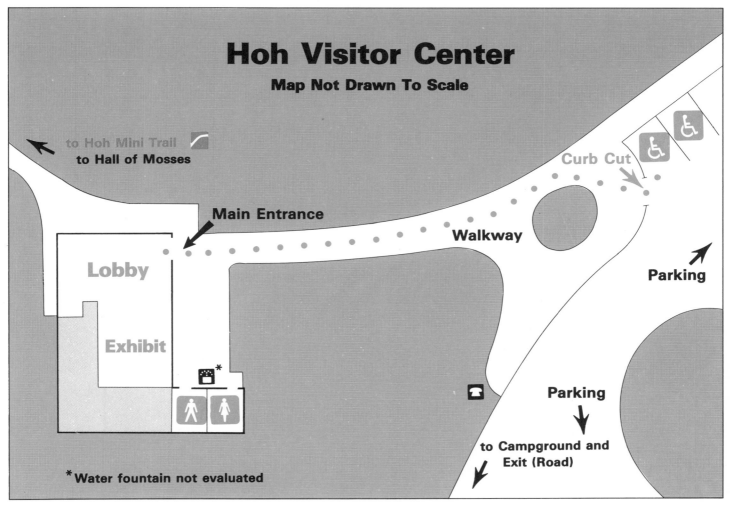

Hoh Visitor Center
Map Not Drawn To Scale

to Hoh Mini Trail
to Hall of Mosses

Main Entrance

Lobby

Exhibit

Curb Cut

Walkway

Parking

Parking

to Campground and Exit (Road)

*Water fountain not evaluated

• The water fountain in front of the restrooms is reported to be accessible.

• A public telephone is located on the path to the restrooms. It may not be accessible.

Hurricane Ridge Lodge

• This building serves as a Visitor Center year round. It also contains a concession-operated food service and gift shop during the summer and winter seasons and ski rentals during the winter season.

• A designated parking area is adjacent to the lodge. The parking area and the sidewalk in front of the main entrance are at the same level, with no curb.

• A ramp to the lower level is in use. A short ramp is also in use from the parking area to the upper level entrance. It is located at the main entrance doorway. Both ramps are reported to have grades less than 1:12.

• An elevator is available and is usable.

Assistance by the staff is required to direct the visitor to the elevator and, since elevator is not usually in use, to activate it.

• There are accessible unisex restrooms on both the upper and lower levels.

• The water fountains are reported to be accessible.

Campgrounds

The campgrounds at Olympic National Park have not been evaluated in relation to UFAS. The following campgrounds have features which are reported "accessible" as listed:

Dosewallips - "Accessible" restrooms.
Elwha - "Accessible" pit toilet.
Fairholm - "Accessible" restroom in Loop B.
Grave's Creek - "Accessible" pit toilet.
Heart O'The Hills - One designated "accessible" site. "Accessible" restroom in Loop A.

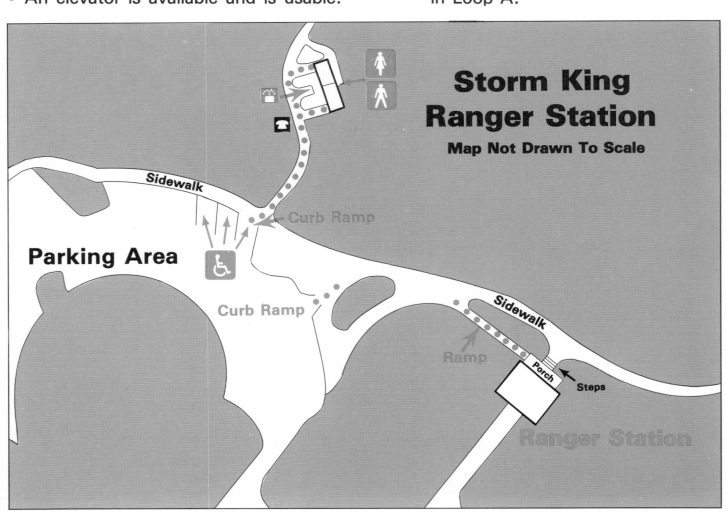

**Storm King
Ranger Station**

Map Not Drawn To Scale

Sidewalk

Curb Ramp

Parking Area

Curb Ramp

Ramp

Sidewalk

Porch

Steps

Ranger Station

Hurricane Ridge Lodge
(Upper Floor)
Map Not Drawn To Scale

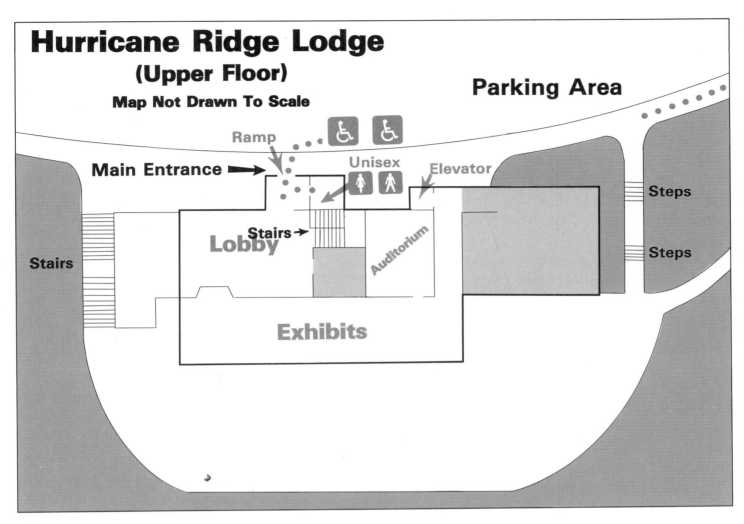

Hurricane Ridge Lodge
(Lower Floor)
Map Not Drawn To Scale

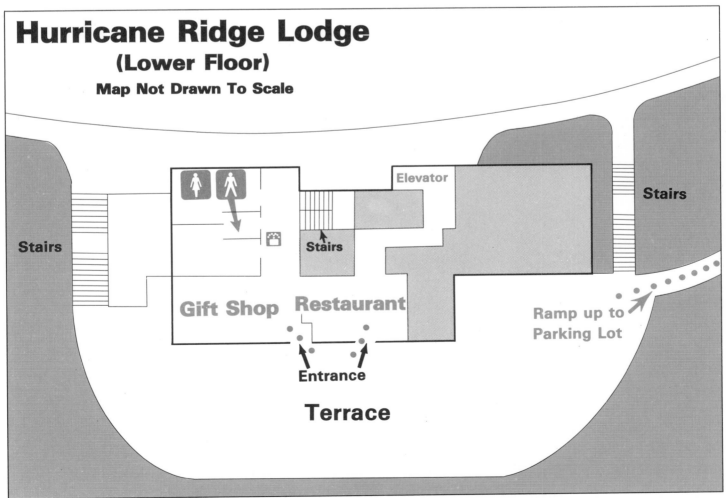

Hoh - "Accessible" restroom in Loop A. Nearly all campsites are flat and potentially accessible.

Kalaloch - Restrooms in Loops A and C may have wide stalls, but no grab bars. All campsites are "borderline accessible".

Mora - "Accessible" restrooms at the campground and at Rialto Beach. All campsites are flat and potentially accessible.

North Fork - "Accessible" restrooms at the Ranger Station. The campsite near the outhouse is wide and flat.

Ozette - "Accessible" restrooms at the Ranger Station.

Queets - "Accessible" pit toilets.

Soleduck - "Accessible" pit toilet. Some campsites in Loop A are flat and may be adequate for some wheelchair users.

Staircase - "Accessible" restroom. Some campsites may be "borderline accessible".

Supplementary Information

• **Kalaloch Lodge** (P.O. Box 1100, Forks, WA 98331) offers lodging and food service in park. A published source reports the following: "Handicapped Facilities - Food service, less severely handicapped can use facility but wheelchair travelers must enter dining room through sliding doors from outside. Lodging, yes. Grocery sales, yes. Reserved parking, no. One large log cabin (with 2 queen-size beds) has been designed for handicapped person in a wheelchair. It features a Jacuzzi pool in the bath." No other details furnished by concessionaire.

An unpublished internal Park survey notes that access to the lodge main entrance has three steps; one step around back to the dining area. Restrooms have 22-inch wide doors. The gift shop has three steps inside; access may be possible from the sliding door in back. The restaurant has two steps inside. Access in the coffee shop is fair. There are no steps inside. "Accessible cabin" has an unbeveled threshold. The jacuzzi lacks grab bars and its controls are positioned too high. Cabins 3, 14 and 35 have no steps but bathroom doors are too narrow.

Note: This survey was done in 1981, so the information may be dated.

• **Fairholm General Store** (HC 62, Box 15, Port Angeles, WA 98362) is a retail store selling camping supplies, fishing gear, firewood, ice and gas. It also has boat rentals and a snack bar. The staff has been sensitized to the needs of patrons with disabilities and has experience serving patrons with mobility impairments (wheelchair users) and developmental disabilities. Group visitation by patrons with disabilities will present no problems.

There is no reserved parking but the surface of the parking area is reported to be level, smooth asphalt. A passenger loading zone adjacent to the entrance is reported to be usable. The route of travel is at least three feet wide over an asphalt or wooden surface; abrupt changes in level are reported to be beveled. A permanent ramp provides access to the store. The ramp is four feet wide with a three-foot edging. Its surface is composed of wooden cross-slats. Its gradient was not reported, so assistance may be required.

Aisles within the store are at least 36 inches wide and are kept free of extruding displays and inventory. The maximum shelf height is seven feet. The check-out aisle is at least 36 inches wide but the sales counter is positioned at an inappropriate height for a wheelchair user. The staff is willing to assist patrons with disabilities: "Can help wheelchairs and blind in store."

A unisex restroom is reported to be on a usable path of travel. The doorway is at least 32 inches wide. The restroom is reported to have a five-foot clear space and usable sink but frontal use from wheelchair is not possible because of inadequate clearance. Hot water pipes are insulated. Properly positioned grab bars are not present.

• **National Park Concessions, Inc.** operates **Hurricane Ridge Lodge** and **Lake Crescent Lodge** (HC 62, Box 11, Port Angeles, WA 98362) Hurricane Ridge Lodge is a day-use facility only. It offers food, gifts and photo supplies. (It also contains a Visitor Center—see *Visitor Centers* section.) A published source reports the following: "Handicapped Facilities - Hurricane Ridge is accessible." Lake Crescent Lodge offers lodging and food. Published source reports "Lake Crescent Lodge lobby, dining room and gift shop are accessible. Rooms have limited accessibility."

• **Sol Duc Hot Springs Resort** (P.O. Box 2169, Port Angeles, WA 98368) offers lodging, dining and hot mineral baths in the park. Published source reports the following: "Handicapped Facilities - Available for pool areas. On-duty life guards assist handicapped into water." No other details furnished by concessionaire.

Basic Facilities

	Restroom	Water Fountain	Telephone
Dosewallips Campground	●		
Elwha Campground	●		
Fairholm Campground	●		
Graves Creek Campground	●		
Heart O'the Hills Campground	●		
Hoh Mini Trail	●	●	
Hoh Visitor Center	●		●
Hurricane Ridge Lodge	●	●	
Kalaloch Campground	●		
Kalaloch Lodge	●		
Mora Campground	●		
North Fork Campground	●		
Ozette Campground	●		
Pioneer Memorial Museum	●	●	●
Queets Campground	●		
Soleduck Campground	●		
Staircase Campground	●		
Storm King Ranger Station	●	●	

As the rugged beauty of this coastline testifies, Redwood N.P. has more to offer than "tall trees."

Redwood

Redwood National Park
1111 Second Street
Crescent City, CA 95531
Tel./TDD (707) 464-6101
See TDD section for instructions.

Redwood National Park and three associated California state parks function together to preserve a remnant of the fragile and unique coastal redwood environment. The majestic redwoods, a part of the sequoia family, grow taller than any other type of tree. The tallest known tree in the world is a redwood in the Tall Trees Grove which is 367.8 feet high. The awesome sense of power these huge trees impart may be felt while being among them on park trails or while driving on Route 101 through the forest.

Millions of years ago the Earth's climate was mild and moist; redwood species dominated the forests over much of the northern hemisphere. The redwood's range is now limited to the coast of northern California and southern Oregon.

These towering trees can grow on the north coast of California because of the environment the Pacific Coast provides. The climate here is moderate throughout the year, and the moisture of the ocean is carried inland in the form of rain and fog. The airborne moisture slows the rate at which the trees lose water due to transpiration. The trees themselves help to perpetuate this moist environment by calming the air, like a windbreak, and trapping cool air near the ground.

The importance of the fog to the health of the redwood trees becomes evident when it fails to form. The Tall Trees Grove is situated in a river valley the slopes of which have been clear-cut for lumber. Without trees on the slopes to help trap the fog, it forms only at the bottom of the valley. As a result, the tops of the tallest trees are dying.

The scenic coast is a great place to watch a sunset, listen to the surf pound on the sandy beach or see a myriad of birds comb the shore. Gray whales, porpoises, seals and sea lions are some of the marine mammals that might be seen offshore. Freshwater lagoons present yet another interesting environment to explore. There is an incredible diversity of wildlife living in the forest, freshwater, marine, and intertidal habitats in this national park.

Climate Chart

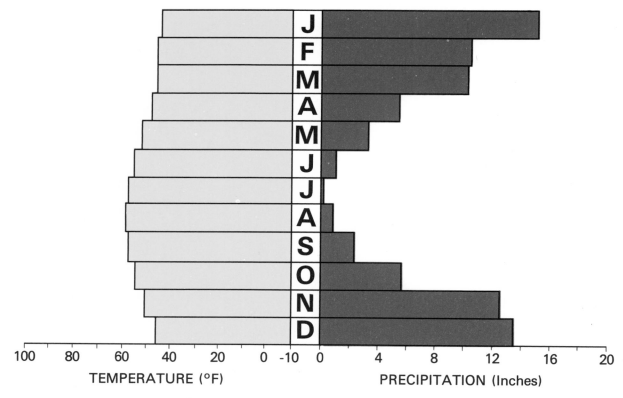

Station Location: Klamath, California
Station Elevation: 25 feet

General Information

Weather

In summer the inland part of the park is warmer than the coast. Inland, July temperatures range from the 70's °F to the 90's. On the coast July temperatures usually range from the 50's to the 60's. Precipitation may be heavy at times, but the summer season is the driest time of the year.

Winter Visitation

The park is open for winter visitation. Programs may vary seasonally, so visitors should check in advance.

Safety

On the beach be aware of tidal fluctuations. Swimming is not advised because the ocean is cold and has a strong undertow. Watch for poison oak, particularly in wintertime. Roosevelt elk are wild and unpredictable—do not approach them on foot.

On the road, watch for logging trucks and other heavy vehicles. Drive cautiously in fog.

Elevation

Elevations of park roads range up to 1000 feet.

Medical and Support Services

The nearest hospitals are located in Crescent City, Arcata and Grants Pass, California. The nearest complete range of services can be found in Eureka and Redding, south of the park.

Publications

• "Access Redwood National Park" is a 12-page booklet addressing accessibility for visitors with mobility, auditory and visual disabilities. It is available on request at all visitor contact points within the park or by writing to the park.

Medical and Support Services

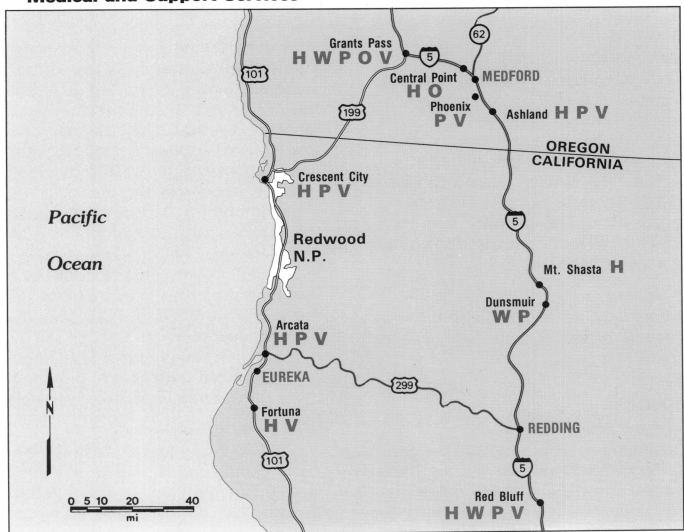

• Another useful publication for visitors to the area is "A Guide to County Regional Parks in the State of California for Persons with Disabilities." It may be obtained by writing:

California Governor's Committee
 for the Employment of the
 Handicapped
P.O. Box 942880
Sacramento, CA 94280

Transportation

• Private vehicles may be used for transportation and visiting some of the park features. Road restrictions on RVs and large trailers may apply. Visitors should check with park personnel.

• Public shuttle buses operate within the park. The shuttle bus tour takes four hours and includes three miles of hiking to the Tall Trees Grove. A 30-minute interpretive talk about the park's history is part of the shuttle bus tour. Shuttle buses are reported to accommodate the needs of visitors with mobility impairments and to be accessible. No details about access have been furnished. Inquire in advance at Redwood Information Center where tickets can be purchased.

Sign Language Interpreter

• Park staff skilled in sign language interpretation are not currently on line. Such personnel may be hired seasonally but their presence cannot be guaranteed each year. The park has not made any pre-arrangements for contacting a sign language interpreter in the event of an emergency.

• It may be possible to arrange program interpretation using sign language, given sufficient advanced notice. Such arrangements would be subject to staff availability and budgetary constraints.

TDD

Redwood National Park has TDD service but there is no dedicated line. The TDD can be operated by calling the Redwood N.P. phone, (707) 464-6101. The caller should tap the space bar for about ten seconds to alert the receptionist to activate the TDD system. Callers can also dial 1-800-342-5966 to reach a California TDD operator. The operator can then transfer the call to the park or to any other TDD number in the state.

Dog Guides

Visitors may use dog guides in the routine course of visiting park features and programs.

Programs

Organized Programs

• Interpreters at **Hiouchi Ranger Station, Park Headquarters** and the **Redwood Information Center** utilize descriptive concrete language in their presentations. Items that can be touched are used in the interpretive delivery.

• Most presentations include the use of simple photographs, pictorial illustration and simple verbal analogies. Special arrangements for interpretation to groups or individuals with developmental disabilities are possible.

• At **Hiouchi Ranger Station** programming consists of information and orientation. Summer interpretive activities include natural history talks and nature walks. This Ranger Station is accessible (see *Visitor Centers* section for details).

• **Headquarters Information Center** in Crescent City is staffed by naturalists who are available to provide information about program schedules and to answer visitors' questions. An eight-minute audio/slide program is available. Publications by the Redwood Natural History Association are on sale. There is no reserved parking. The

building is accessible but restrooms are not (see *Visitor Centers* section for details).

• In the Orick area at the **Redwood Information Center** park personnel are available for orientation and assistance in planning a visit. The Information Center is open all year and is fully accessible. Special features include a three-dimensional map and a hands-on exhibit. A slide program is accessible to wheelchair users. Tickets for the Tall Trees shuttle bus may be purchased here. Information about other recreational opportunities in the Humboldt County area is available from the local Chamber of Commerce which maintains an office in this facility during the summer season.

• Interpretive tours of the Tall Trees area are conducted by a shuttle bus program (see *Transportation* section for details).

State Park Programs

Campfire talks are held daily at the state park campgrounds during the summer season. In the Hiouchi area, **Jedediah Smith Redwoods State Park** Campground's program is accessible with reserved parking, accessible restrooms and water supply available on-site. South of Crescent City, in the Del Norte Coast Redwoods State Park, the campground at **Mill Creek** has an accessible interpretive program with reserved parking and accessible restrooms and water supply available on-site. Allowances for wheelchairs have been made in the seating for the campfire talks held at both campgrounds.

Self-Guided Programs

• **Coastal Drive** southeast of Klamath is an 8-mile alternate route paralleling Route 101. RVs and large trailers are not recommended on this partially paved road. Wayside stops have been explicitly designed for viewing from a vehicle, with the exception of Gold Bluffs Beach Overlook. Superb scenery, native wildflowers

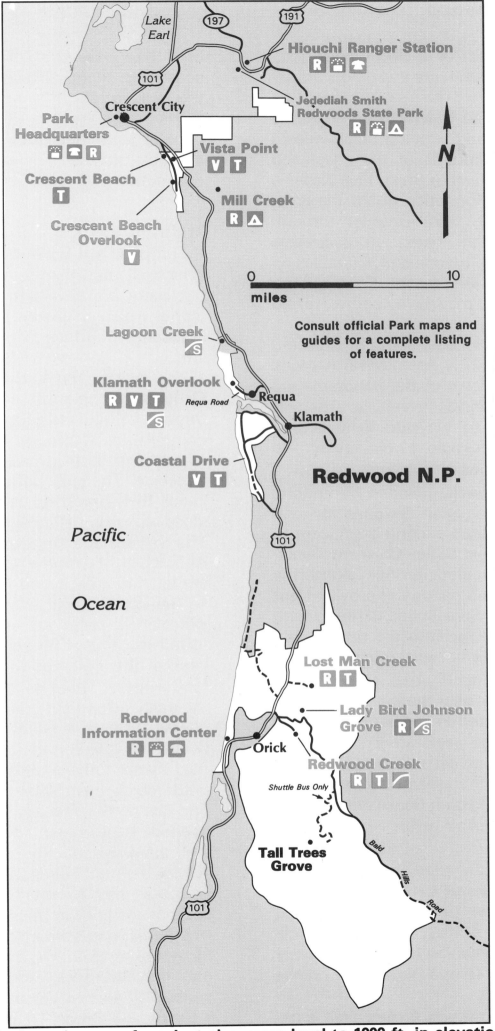

Lake
Earl

197   191

Hiouchi Ranger Station
R 🏠 🏕

Crescent City

Jedediah Smith
Redwoods State Park
R 🏠 ⛺

Park
Headquarters
🏠 🏕 R

101

Vista Point
V T

Crescent Beach
T

Mill Creek
R ⛺

Crescent Beach
Overlook
V

N

0   10
miles

Consult official Park maps and
guides for a complete listing
of features.

Lagoon Creek
S

Klamath Overlook
R V T
S

Requa

Requa Road

Klamath

Coastal Drive
V T

Redwood N.P.

101

Pacific

Ocean

Lost Man Creek
R T

Redwood
Information Center
R 🏠 🏕

Lady Bird Johnson
Grove R S

Orick

Redwood Creek
R T

Shuttle Bus Only

Tall Trees
Grove

Bald

Hills

Road

101

Park roads range from just above sea level to 1000 ft. in elevation.

and the prospect of seeing whales (October through June) are this road's attractions.

• Requa Road to **Klamath Overlook** is narrow, steep and winding. It provides a spectacular panorama of the coast and mouth of the Klamath River. Five wayside exhibits give information about the area. Whale-watching from October through June is excellent here. An accessible grassy area with modified picnic tables on a concrete pad are present. Chemical toilets are accessible by paved pathways and ramp.

• **Vista Point**, located south of Crescent City on Route 101, has several wayside exhibits. Full views of the panorama are possible from inside a vehicle. There is paved access to wayside exhibits and wheelchair accessible picnic tables. No restroom facilities are present.

• **Crescent Beach**, reached by Enderts Beach Road, has been designed for total access. Designated parking is adjacent to a modified picnic table. Crescent Beach Overlook is located further along the road. Designated parking is provided but wheelchair users are limited to the parking area. Restroom facilities are present but accessibility was not evaluated.

• **Lost Man** Picnic Area features five wayside exhibits near the trailhead. Picnic tables are situated in a quiet stream-side area. Wheelchair users are likely to need assistance. Chemical toilets serving the picnic area are themselves accessible but the surface of the path (loose wood chips) requires wheelchair users to have assistance.

• There are picnic sites near the parking lot at the **Redwood Creek** trailhead. No water is available. Chemical toilets do not comply with UFAS. Fully accessible chemical toilets can be found at the **Lady Bird Johnson Grove** parking lot on the Bald Hills Road.

• **Lady Bird Johnson Grove** Trail is described in a self-guiding booklet. (For a brief description see *Trails*, below.) Fully-accessible chemical toilets are located at the parking lot.

• The Yurok Trail is a self-guiding trail. A booklet with descriptive information is available at the trailhead. (For a brief description see *Trails* section.)

Trails

• The park has no trails that have been specifically designed for wheelchair users but there are several trails or trail segments which might be feasible with the assistance of a fully ambulatory companion.

• The trail at the **Lady Bird Johnson Grove** might be accessed with assistance through self-guided Stop #9. The trail is a one-mile loop through old-growth redwoods and is an excellent area for bird watching. The most difficult section is the initial 18% grade up to the bridge and steep incline immediately after the bridge. The trail surface has exposed tree roots. Accessible restrooms (chemical toilets) are located adjacent to the parking lot.

• The Yurok Trail is a 0.8-mile loop. Wheelchair users are recommended to have assistance. The trail surface is hard-packed dirt. Rain can make the trail surface slippery. There is flat terrain between the trailhead and the bridge. The trail then passes through a relatively flat meadow where the trail surface becomes bumpy. Past a small grove of alders there is a 15% grade climb (very short segment) to the first overlook. The trail to the second overlook is less steep. At the second overlook there are tidal pool and sea exhibits. A wide variety of birds abounds and there is opportunity to watch whales, harbor seals or sea lions in the surf. The balance of the trail (one-third mile) has a challenging grade of 15%. The trail surface is firm and gravelly. Trail width has been described as narrow but passable.

• **Redwood Creek** Trail may be negotiable with assistance for the first 1.5 miles

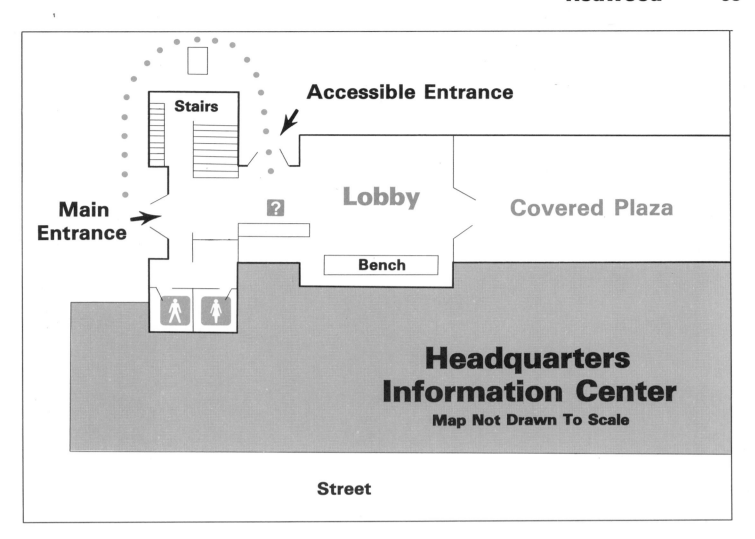

Headquarters
Information Center
Map Not Drawn To Scale

(to the river crossing). Accessibility depends on the weather and trail maintenance conditions.

Exhibits

• For references to wayside exhibits see *Self-Guiding Programs* and *Trails* above.

• General information about the park is available in well-illustrated or pictorial formats.

 • An eight-minute audio/slide show is available at the Chamber of Commerce and the **Redwood Information Center**. The show describes area campgrounds and gives a brief park history.

• In general, all park exhibits have been designed to be accessible to wheelchair users. At the **Hiouchi Ranger Station**, park exhibits and book sales are displayed low enough to be fully accessible to wheelchair users.

• Exhibit design employs the use of adequate, even lighting, high-contrast colors on photographs and non-glare glass. Exhibit lettering is not routed or raised.

• A three-dimensional park map is available for tactile interpretation at the **Redwood Information Center**.

Visitor Centers

Headquarters Information Center

• Located one block off Highway 101 at 2nd and K Streets in Crescent City.

• There is no reserved parking at this time. Parking is controlled by the city. Requests have been made for marked reserved spaces. Generally, parking is about half a block from the Information Center. Accessible curb cuts from the street to the sidewalk are reported.

• The sidewalk is reported to be accessible and is level and smooth concrete.

• The information desk is positioned low enough for wheelchair users. Informa-

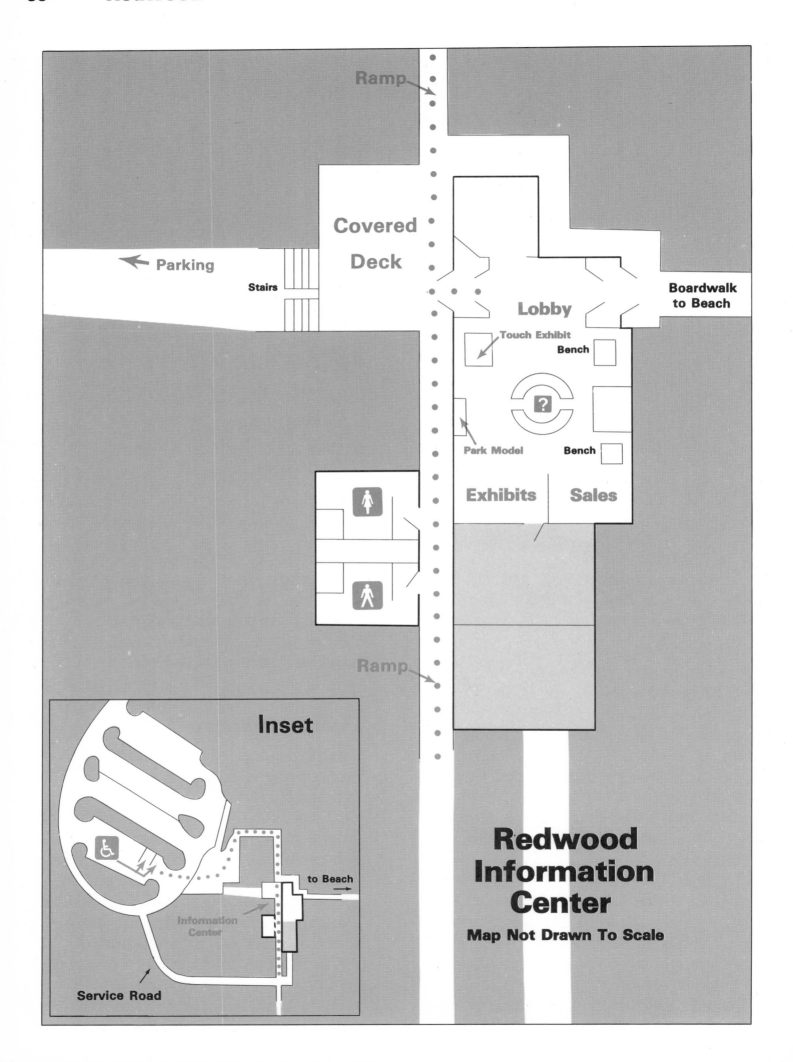

Ramp

Covered

Deck

← Parking

Stairs

Boardwalk to Beach

Lobby

Touch Exhibit

Bench

Park Model

Bench

Exhibits   Sales

Ramp

Inset

Information Center

to Beach

Service Road

Redwood
Information
Center
Map Not Drawn To Scale

tional materials are placed within a 24-inch reach on the desk.
- Restrooms do not meet all UFAS but they are usable. Space in the stalls is limited, so some wheelchair users may need assistance. Other features, including door swing, grab bars and entryways, have been remodeled to meet standards.
- The water fountain is accessible. The spout allows for use of a cup and the operating lever moves easily.
- There is no accessible public telephone at this Information Center.
- TDD service is available. (See *TDD* section for details.)

Redwood Information Center
- Located on Highway 101, two miles south of the town of Orick.
- This new building has been designed for total accessibility. It is open year round.
- There is reserved, signed, accessible parking about 200 feet from the Information Center. The parking area is paved, level and smooth. There is a passenger loading zone about 175 feet from the Information Center. The loading zone is concrete, level and smooth. Accessible curb cuts are in place.
- There is a continuous accessible route of travel from the parking area to the side entrance. The pathway is asphalt and redwood and is level and smooth. A ramp in use on this route has a grade less than 1:12. It is equipped with handrails, edging, and an all-weather, non-slip surface.
- The entrance on the opposite side of the building is also accessible.
- The information desk is accessible to wheelchair users. Informational materials are placed within a 24-inch reach on the desk.
- The restrooms in the Redwood Information Center are fully accessible to wheelchair users. Faucets are also easy to turn.
- The water fountain is accessible to wheelchair users. The spout allows for use of a cup and the lever is easy to turn.

- The public telephone is accessible to wheelchair users. It does not have a volume control but it is hearing-aid compatible.

Hiouchi Ranger Station
- Located on Highway 199, ten miles northeast of Crescent City. It is open during summer only.
- There is reserved, accessible parking approximately 90 feet from the Ranger Station. The reserved spaces do not have signs at present. The parking area is paved, level and smooth.
- There is a continuous accessible route of travel from the parking area to the main entrance of the Ranger Station. The pathway is asphalt and redwood deck. It is reported to be level and smooth. There is a ramp in place on this route. Its grade is 3.5%. It is equipped with handrails, edging, and an all-weather, non-slip surface.
- The information desk is designed to be accessible to wheelchair users. Informational materials are placed within a 24-inch reach on the desk. An excellent selection of books, posters and exhibits is displayed low enough to be visible and accessible from a wheelchair.
- The restrooms in the Hiouchi Ranger Station are fully accessible.
- The water fountain is accessible to wheelchair users. The spout allows for use of a cup and the lever moves easily.
- The public telephone is reported to be accessible but it may be too high for some wheelchair users. This telephone does not have a volume control and it is not hearing-aid compatible.

Campgrounds
There are no National Park Service Campgrounds in Redwood National Park. Campgrounds are available in the three associated California State Parks.

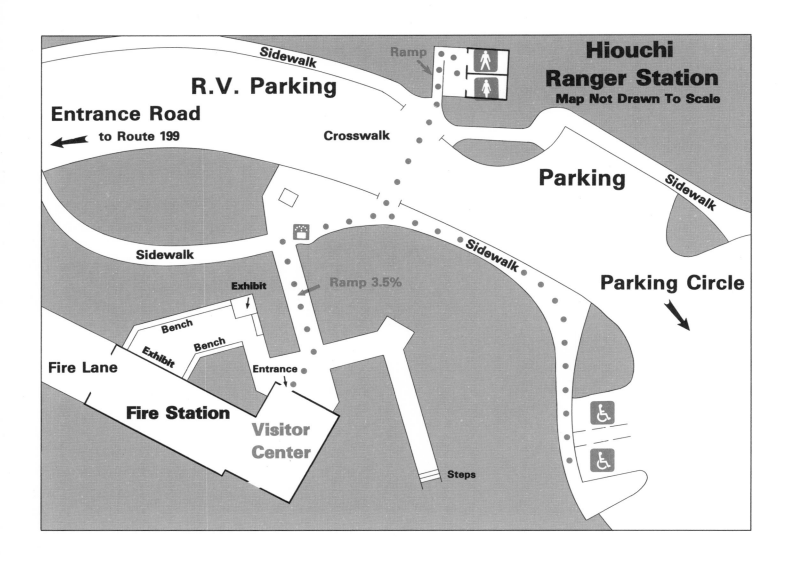

Basic Facilities

	Restroom	Water Fountain	Telephone
Hiouchi Ranger Station	●	●	●
Jedediah Smith Redwoods State Park	●	●	
Klamath Overlook	●		
Lady Bird Johnson Grove	●		
Lost Man	●		
Mill Creek Campground	●		
Park Headquarters	●	●	●
Redwood Creek	●		
Redwood Information Center	●	●	●

Sequoia
and
Kings
Canyon

Sequoia/Kings Canyon
Chief Park Interpreter
National Park Service
Sequoia/Kings Canyon N.P.'s
Three Rivers, CA 93271
Tel. (209) 565-3341

Sequoia and Kings Canyon National Parks encompass a large stretch of the crest of the Sierra Nevada Mountains as well as a slightly lower intermediate crest known as the Great Western Divide. These parks contain Mt. Whitney, the highest mountain in the continental United States (14,495 feet), and the General Sherman sequoia, the largest living thing on earth.

The General Sherman Tree, perhaps 2200 years old, is the largest giant sequoia. The weight of its trunk is estimated to be 1385 tons. Its height is 274.9 feet, its circumference at the ground 102.6 feet and the diameter of its largest branch is 6.8 feet.

These two parks offer the visitor spectacular scenery from towering forests to high mountain peaks. Glacial lakes and cold mountain streams are everywhere. Most of the areas in the parks are accessible by foot trail only and no road passes completely through from east to west.

Sequoia and Kings Canyon National Parks are part of the International Man and the Biosphere program to conserve genetic diversity and maintain an environmental baseline for research and monitoring.

General Information
Weather

In mid-summer at lower elevations temperatures range from lows in the 70's to highs near 100°F. At the middle elevations they range from lows in the 50's to highs in the upper 80's. Most of the precipitation occurs in the winter.

Winter Visitation

The parks are open for winter visitation. There is deep snow and some park roads are routinely closed; others may be closed temporarily due to weather conditions. At times, tire chains may be mandatory. Accessibility in the winter is difficult because of deep snow. Even though some paths are shoveled, visitors with diabilities probably will require assistance.

Safety

Be cautious near park waters, especially during the spring. Drive winding roads with care. Thunderstorms pose lightning hazards—stay in your car or cabin. Learn to identify and avoid poison oak; it is likely to be found in moist woodland, brushland and along creeks.

Climate Charts

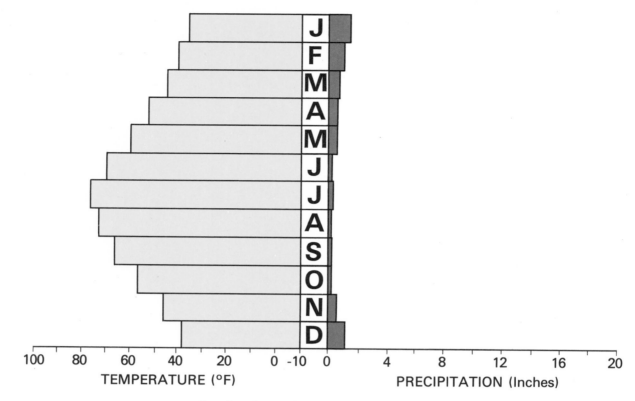

TEMPERATURE (°F)   PRECIPITATION (Inches)

Station Location: Bishop, California
Station Elevation: 4108 feet

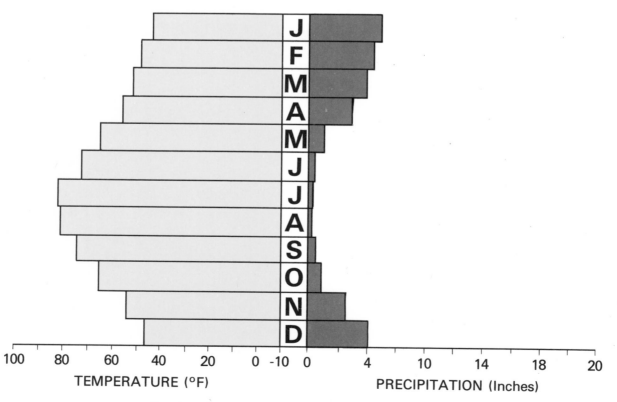

TEMPERATURE (°F)   PRECIPITATION (Inches)

Station Location: Ash Mountain, California
Station Elevation: 2140 feet

Medical and Support Services

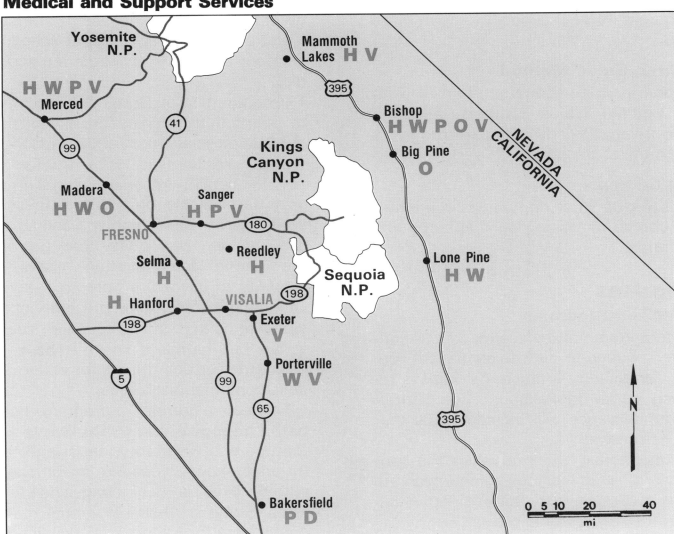

Elevation

The elevation of roads in the parks ranges from 1700 feet to 7000 feet. Thin air at high elevations may aggravate heart or respiratory problems.

Medical and Support Services

The nearest complete range of services can be found in Visalia and Fresno, California, west of the park. The nearest hospitals are located in Reedley (for Kings Canyon N.P.) and Exeter (for Sequoia N.P.).

Publications

• "National Park Service, Sequoia and Kings Canyon National Parks: Access" is a single sheet chart that highlights accessible park features and programs. Inquire at visitor centers or write to the park.
• "Sequoia Bark" is the park newspaper.

In addition to general program schedules and information, accessible park features and programs are identified by the international symbol of accessibility.

Transportation

• Private cars can be used for transportation in visiting park features and programs. Over one-hundred miles of main roads are maintained in the parks.
• Concessionaires offer tours via van and bus. There appear to be no special provisions for accommodating the needs of visitors with disabilities.

Sign Language Interpreter

There are no park staff with sign language interpretation skills. The parks have no pre-arrangements for contacting a sign language interpreter in the event of an emergency.

TDD

There is no TDD capability within these parks.

Sighted Guide Method

Some park personnel are familiar with the Sighted Guide Method, although there are no regularly scheduled programs which utilize this skill.

Dog Guides

Visitors may use dog guides in the routine course of visiting park features and programs.

Programs

Organized Programs

Interpreters utilize descriptive and concrete language to discuss significant scenery, landmarks, artifacts or displays requiring visual appreciation. Some interpretive deliveries will include items that can be touched.

Programming which involves the handling of objects includes some which are on an accessible work surface and within a 24-inch reach; some are not.

A portion of the slide presentation program has been captioned.

• The **Lodgepole Visitor Center** programming, consists of orientation, information, exhibits and publication sales. This Visitor Center is accessible (see *Visitor Centers* section for details). The auditorium is also accessible and allowances are made for wheelchair users in the seating area. Presentations are given about natural history, plant and animal life and forest fire fighting techniques. Some of the presentations include items that can be touched, such as the fur of a bear.

• The **Lodgepole Amphitheater**, located in the middle of the campground, is reported as "marginally accessible" because of steep grades. Assistance would be required. Allowances are made for wheelchair users in the seating area. A campfire program and an interactive pro-

gram about park management are given. Visitors should check current schedules. Outdoor exhibits in this area are accessible.

• Programming at **Grant Grove** consists of orientation, information, exhibits and publication sales. Most of the Visitor Center is accessible (see *Visitor Centers* section for detail). An orientation slide program is available on request. Presentations about photography, animal life, park history and policy are given. A fire-fighting demonstration allows participants to use a fire hose to spray out an imaginary fire. Some presentations include items that can be touched, such as a live but harmless snake. These programs may be appropriate for visitors with developmental disabilities.

• There are a number of programs held at both **Lodgepole** and **Grant Grove** areas that are addressed to younger audiences (puppet shows, roasting marshmallows with Smokey the Bear, songs and stories, etc.). Some of these programs may be appropriate for visitors with developmental disabilities. Visitors should check program schedules and inquire for details.

• The campfire programs at **Sunset Campground** are accessible. Films and slide shows about Sequoia and Kings Canyon are presented.

• The Grant Tree Walk is a one-hour presentation. The group meets at **Grant Tree** parking area. Assistance may be required. There is designated parking. The water fountain and restrooms have been modified for use by visitors with disabilities. The site has not been evaluated in relation to UFAS.

• An interpretive talk about Indian life is held at the ramada (a shelter) adjacent to the post office at **Grant Grove** Village. The ramada is accessible to wheelchair users.

• The **Cedar Grove Amphitheater** is accessible.

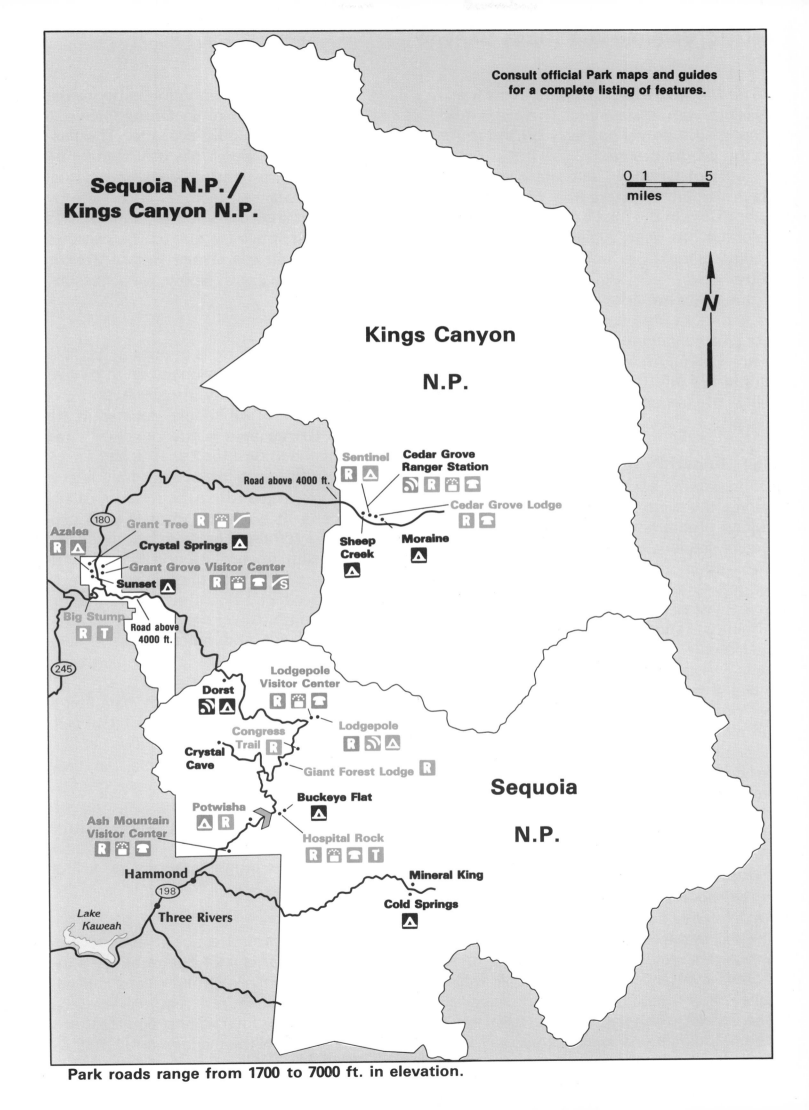

**Sequoia N.P. /
Kings Canyon N.P.**

Consult official Park maps and guides
for a complete listing of features.

0 1 5
miles

N

Kings Canyon

N.P.

Sentinel
Road above 4000 ft.

Cedar Grove
Ranger Station

Cedar Grove Lodge

180
Grant Tree
Azalea

Crystal Springs

Grant Grove Visitor Center

Sheep
Creek

Moraine

Sunset

Big Stump

Road above
4000 ft.

245

Lodgepole
Visitor Center

Dorst

Congress
Trail

Lodgepole

Crystal
Cave

Giant Forest Lodge

Sequoia

Potwisha

Buckeye Flat

N.P.

Ash Mountain
Visitor Center

Hospital Rock

Hammond

Mineral King

198

Cold Springs

Three Rivers

Lake
Kaweah

Park roads range from 1700 to 7000 ft. in elevation.

• The **Mineral King** Campfire Circle is accessible with assistance. There are two steps and a gravel pathway on the route to the program area.

• Tours of **Crystal Cave** are given. The Cave is open to visitors from May through Labor Day. In the past a sign language interpreter has been available for the tour. Visitors should ask about current availability.

• Bus tours are conducted daily (subject to minimum sign-up) by private concession. Tours include the Kings Canyon and Giant Forest Areas. Reservations are required. No information about the accessibility of transportation has been furnished.

Self-Guided Programs

• Park roads, some of which are closed during the winter, are the basis of self-guided programming in the parks. Spectacular scenery is observable from the car, with additional views requiring passengers to leave their vehicle at turnouts. Some vistas and attractions are located within a "short walk . . . along well-developed and maintained paths or trails." Assistance may be required.

• **Big Stump** Picnic Area is reported to be "potentially accessible". There are dirt pathways which may have steep grades. Assistance is likely required. There is designated parking with curb cuts. The restrooms and picnic tables have been modified to accommodate visitors using wheelchairs. Modifications may not meet UFAS.

• **Hospital Rock** Picnic Area is reported to be accessible. There is designated parking with curb cuts to the walkway. The trail in the area is paved. The building is reported to be accessible. The restrooms, a water fountain and picnic table have been modified for visitors using wheelchairs. The telephone has been lowered. Modifications in this area may not all meet UFAS.

• Self-guiding information about the "Trail for All People" in **Grant Grove** is available on an audio cassette. The cassette has been specifically designed for visitors who are blind or who have visual disabilities. It has been tested on-site by staff or blind consultants and utilizes highly descriptive language. The cassette is available at the **Grant Grove Visitor Center**. (See *Trails*, below, for accessibility.)

Trails

• In general, park trails are not accessible to visitors using wheelchairs or who have other serious mobility impairments.

• The "Trail for All People" located in the **Grant Grove** area is the only park trail that has been designed specifically for visitors with disabilities. The trail has a blacktop surface with a minimum width of 36 inches. It contrasts visually with surrounding terrain. The trail has extended grades that do not exceed 5%. At the trailhead printed or signed information is available which relates such information as trail length, travel time, degree of difficulty, facilities and precautions. A self-guiding audio cassette is available at the **Grant Grove Visitor Center**.

• Three trails are identified by park literature as being potentially accessible to visitors with disabilities. All should be considered as marginally accessible, as they have dirt surfaces and/or steep grades. These include the **Congress**, Round Meadow and Tharps Log trails. Visitors should inquire about specific requirements at the ranger stations or visitor centers.

Exhibits

• General information about the park environment that is well-illustrated by photographs or other pictorial means is available. Such illustrated material may be appropriate for interpreting park features to individuals with developmental disabilities.

• The **Lodgepole** Nature Center has "hands-on" exhibits. It is open daily from the beginning of July through Labor Day. The Nature Center is self-paced and involves participation. It may be appropriate for visitors with developmental disabilities.

• A few of the parks' signs, labels and exhibits are designed to be accessible to wheelchair users.

• Exhibits on the "Trail for All People" in the **Grant Grove** area have been designed for viewing from a wheelchair (see also *Trails* section, above).

• Most horizontal wayside exhibits located throughout the parks have a minimum of 27 inches of ground clearance and adjacent clear space to allow a frontal approach by a wheelchair user but some may be too high to allow proper viewing (i.e., from eye level of 48 inches).

• Items to be manipulated on exhibits, such as buttons or knobs, are mounted at an accessible height for wheelchair users.

There are only a few exhibits which use this format.

• Audio-visual exhibits at the **Lodgepole** and **Grant Grove Visitor Centers** are accessible.

• All exhibits employ the use of adequate and even lighting. Some interpretive signs are routed.

• Some book sale exhibits may be accessible.

Visitor Centers

Ash Mountain Visitor Center

• Located 8 miles north of Three Rivers, one mile inside Sequoia National Park, at Park Headquarters.

• There is reserved, signed, accessible parking and a passenger loading zone about 75 to 100 feet from the Visitor Center. Accessible curb cuts are in place. The parking area and loading zone are paved, level and smooth.

• There is a continuous accessible route

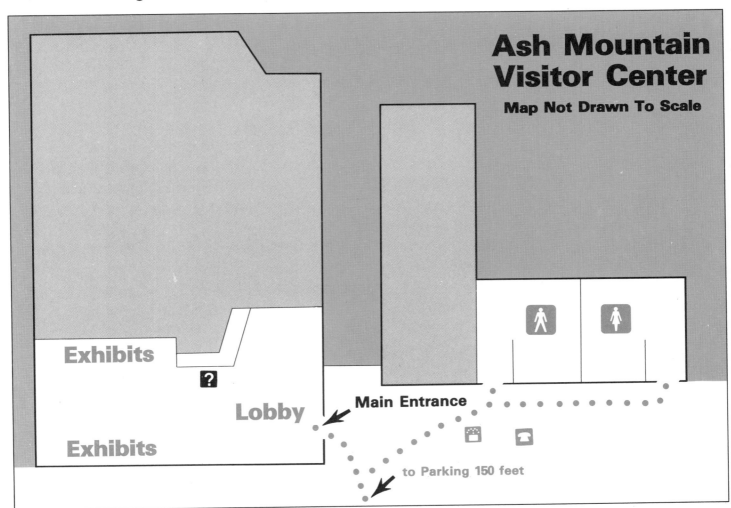

Ash Mountain Visitor Center

Map Not Drawn To Scale

Exhibits

Lobby

Main Entrance

Exhibits

to Parking 150 feet

from the reserved parking to the main entrance and to the restrooms, which have separate entrances. The pathway is concrete, level and smooth.

• The information desk is higher than 34 inches.

• The restrooms have separate entrances located near the main Visitor Center entrance. Both the men's and women's restrooms are fully accessible to wheelchair users.

• The water fountain is located outside in front of the Visitor Center and is accessible. The spout allows for use of a cup and the lever moves easily.

• The telephone is located outside the restrooms in front of the Visitor Center. It is positioned to be accessible to wheelchair users and the telephone has a volume control.

Lodgepole Visitor Center

• This Center is located in the Giant Forest area of Sequoia National Park, about 20 miles north of Park Headquarters.

• There is reserved, signed, accessible parking about 150 feet from the Visitor Center. There is a passenger loading zone adjacent to the Visitor Center. Accessible curb cuts are in place. The parking area and loading zone are paved, level and smooth.

• There is a continuous accessible route from the reserved parking to the main entrance and to the restroom entrances, which are separate. The pathway is concrete, level and smooth. It slopes from the street level to the building level. The grade of this sloped area is less than 1:12.

• The auditorium is accessible and there is space for wheelchairs in the seating area.

• The information desk is higher than 34 inches.

• Restrooms are fully accessible.

• The water fountain is placed at a proper height for wheelchair users. The spout allows for use of a cup.

• The public telephone is located on the outside wall of the Visitor Center. It is

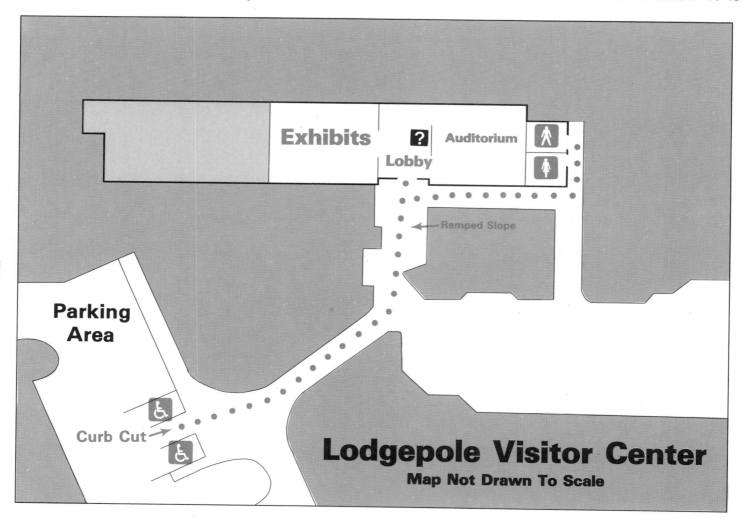

Lodgepole Visitor Center
Map Not Drawn To Scale

placed at a proper height for wheelchair users. The telephone is hearing-aid compatible but it may not have a volume control.

Grant Grove Visitor Center

• Located in the Grant Grove area of Kings Canyon National Park.
• There is reserved, signed, accessible parking and a passenger loading zone 50 to 75 feet from the Visitor Center. The parking area and loading zone are paved, level and smooth. Accessible curb cuts are in place.
• There is a continuous accessible route from the reserved parking to the main entrance and to the restrooms, which have a separate entrance. The pathway is a level concrete sidewalk.
• The information desk is higher than 34 inches.
• Restrooms have separate entrances, near the main entrance to the Visitor Center. Both the men's and women's restrooms are fully accessible.
• The water fountain is located outside the main entrance. It is accessible to wheelchair users. The spout allows for use of a cup.
• The public telephone at the Gift Shop/Restaurant is accessible to wheelchair users but does not have a volume control.

Cedar Grove Ranger Station

• Located in the Cedar Grove area of Kings Canyon National Park. This is a small one-room ranger station which also serves as a Visitor Center.
• There is reserved parking.
• The Ranger Station may be accessible with assistance. The entrance is on ground level, but the door sill may require assistance. There is an outdoor exhibit which is accessible.
• There is no restroom in the ranger station but the restroom nearby in the Sentinel Campground is fully accessible.

• A water fountain and telephone nearby are reported to be accessible.

Campgrounds

Lodgepole Campground

• There is a designated, reserved campsite for visitors with disabilities. The parking surface is level asphalt and concrete. There is an accessible paved pathway from the parking area several feet to the campsite.
• The restrooms are fully accessible.
• The water source is not fully accessible. The faucets do not have adequate clear space to allow approach by a wheelchair user.
• The cooking grill is not positioned between 30 and 36 inches high and there is not adequate clear space for approach by a wheelchair user.
• Reservations for this campground are required and may be made through Ticketron®. Apply in person at any local Ticketron® office, or by mail to:

Ticketron®
Department R
401 Hackensack Ave.
Hackensack, NJ 07601

Potwisha Campground

Note: Potwisha Campground is open during winter.
• Site 39 is designated for visitors with disabilities. Campsites are level.
• Restrooms are reported to be accessible.
• A water fountain is reported to be accessible.
• Picnic tables have been modified for accessibility.

Azalea Campground

• Azalea Campground is located in Grant Grove.
• Site 38 is designated for visitors with disabilities. Parking is several feet from the campsite. The parking surface and a route to the campsite are level asphalt and concrete.

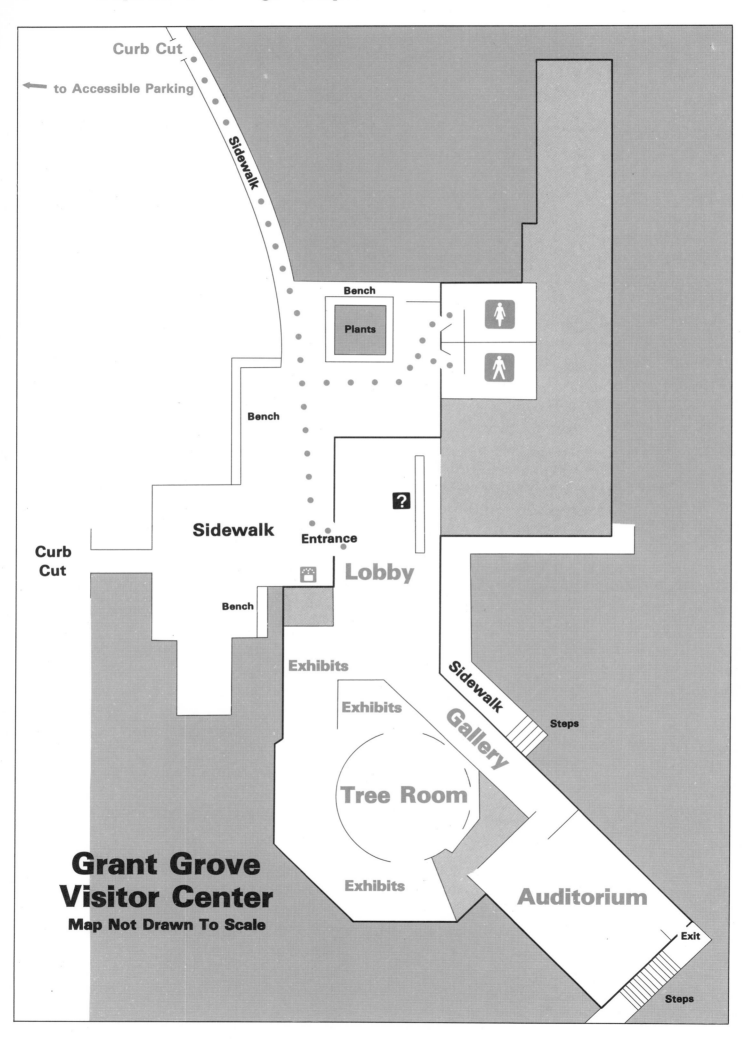

Curb Cut

← to Accessible Parking

Sidewalk

Bench

Plants

Bench

Bench

Sidewalk

Entrance

Curb
Cut

Lobby

Bench

Exhibits

Exhibits

Sidewalk

Gallery

Steps

Tree Room

**Grant Grove
Visitor Center**
Map Not Drawn To Scale

Exhibits

Auditorium

Exit

Steps

• The restrooms are fully accessible.
• The water source, a faucet, is accessible.
• The cooking grill is between 30 and 36 inches high and is accessible. Modified picnic tables are also available.

Sentinel Campground

• Sentinel Campground is located in Cedar Grove.
• Site 10 is designated for visitors with disabilities. Parking is about 20 feet from the campsite. The parking surface is level and paved. There is an accessible paved route of travel from the parking area to the campsite.

• The restrooms are fully accessible.
• The water source is a faucet that does not have adequate clear space to allow approach by a wheelchair user.
• The cooking grill height is not between 30 and 36 inches. There is not adequate clear space to allow approach by a wheelchair user. There are accessible picnic tables.

Sheep Creek, Moraine, Sunset and **Crystal Springs Campgrounds** have no campsites which have been specifically designed or are especially appropriate for visitors with disabilities.

Basic Facilities

	Restroom	Water Fountain	Telephone
Ash Mountain Visitor Center	●	●	●
Azalea Campground	●		
Big Stump	●		
Cedar Grove Lodge	●		●
Cedar Grove Ranger Station	●	●	●
Congress Trail	●		
Giant Forest Lodge	●		
Grant Grove Visitor Center	●	●	●
Grant Tree	●	●	
Hospital Rock	●	●	●
Lodgepole	●		
Lodgepole Visitor Center	●	●	●
Potwisha Campground	●		
Sentinel Campground	●		

Yosemite Valley from Tunnel View.

LAURA FEASTER

Yosemite

Public Information Office
Yosemite National Park
P.O. Box 577
Yosemite N.P., CA 95389
Tel. (209) 372-0265
TDD (209) 372-4726

Yosemite National Park was set aside in 1890 to preserve the scenic wilderness of a portion of the Sierra Nevada mountains. The park ranges in elevation from 2000 feet above sea level to over 13,000 feet and has three major features: alpine wilderness, groves of Giant Sequoia and Yosemite Valley.

Hundreds of millions of years ago the rocks of the Sierra Nevada were uplifted and folded. Simultaneously, molten rock welled up from deep within the earth and cooled slowly to form granite. Over time most of the softer overlying rocks have been eroded away, exposing the granite. Even as the Sierra Range continued to form, water and glaciers went to work carving out the face of Yosemite.

Yosemite Valley is known for its towering cliffs, rounded domes and cascading waterfalls. The Valley is a mixture of open meadow dotted with wildflowers, oak woodlands and mixed conifer forests of ponderosa pine, incense cedar and Douglas fir. Wildlife as diverse as the monarch butterfly, mule deer and black bear flourish here. Behind the Valley Visitor Center the Yosemite Museum and Indian Village commemorate the Native Americans who inhabited the region long before it was "discovered".

There are three groves of Giant Sequoia in the park. The largest, Mariposa Grove, is located 35 miles south of Yosemite Valley. The Tuolumne and Merced Groves are near Crane Flat. Many of these huge trees are more than 2000 years old.

Following California Route 120, Tioga Road, the visitor will get a taste of sub-alpine meadows and the high country. The road passes through an area of sparkling lakes and lofty peaks. There are many scenic pullouts along the route.

In Yosemite National Park the visitor soon discovers that the beautiful and the rare are commonplace.

General Information
Weather
Average monthly summer temperatures at Yosemite are in the 70 to 80°F range. The summer season is dry. Winters can be very cold. Most of the precipitation falls during January and February.

Winter Visitation
The park is open for visitation during

Climate Chart

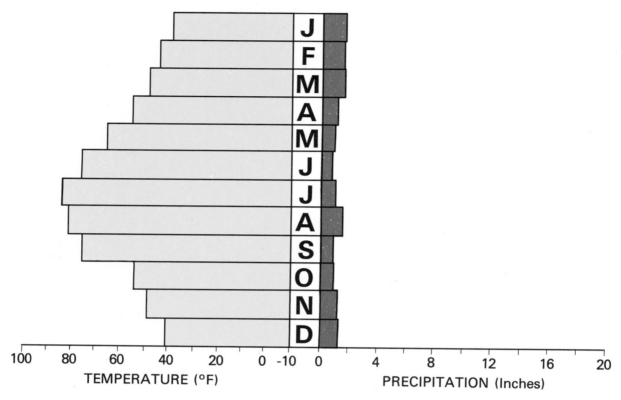

Station Location: Zion N.P.
Station Elevation: 4050 feet

winter. Not all facilities are operative. Road conditions may be hazardous due to snow and ice.

Safety

Take time to read park literature about bear behavior and habitat. Take proper precautions against accidents with bears. Rivers, streams and waterfalls can be treacherous at all times, but especially when water levels are high. Approach them cautiously and be alert for undermined banks and slippery rocks. In case of emergencies call 911.

Elevation

Road elevations range from 3900 feet in the Yosemite Valley area to nearly 10,000 feet in the Tuolumne Meadows area. At Tioga Pass the road crosses the Sierra crest at 9945 feet, the highest automobile pass in California. These high elevations can be dangerous for visitors with heart or respiratory conditions. Caution against overexertion is advised. Visitors may wish to consult their physician before travelling to high elevations.

Medical and Support Services

Yosemite Medical Clinic is located in Yosemite Village. Twenty-four-hour emergency service is available. The Yosemite Dental Clinic is also located in the Valley. Both clinics are privately operated. (See also the *Supplementary Information* section.) The nearest hospitals are located in Mammoth Lakes, California, southeast of the park, and in Mariposa, west of the park. The nearest complete range of services can be found in Sacramento, northwest of the park, and Fresno, south of the park.

Publications

• ''Yosemite Park: Access Information for Disabled Visitors'' (1984 issue reviewed, current issue may be available) is a six-page mimeographed brochure describing

Medical and Support Services

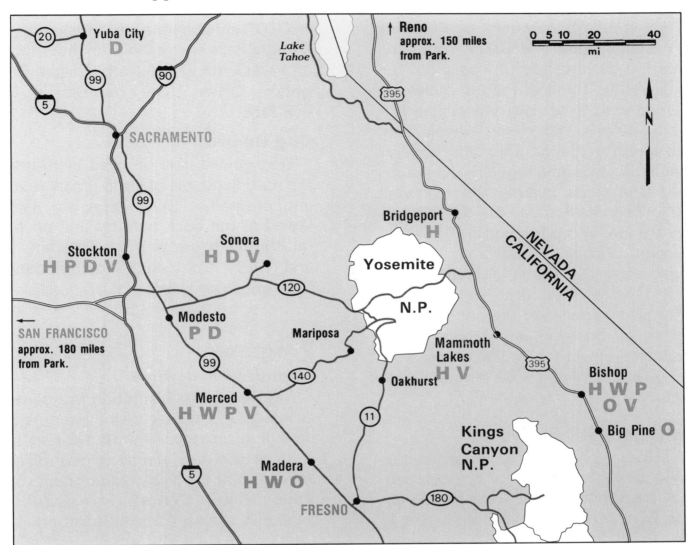

park programs and features of interest to visitors with disabilities. It is available at the entrance or information stations or by writing to the park.

• "Yosemite National Park: Access for Visitors" is a ten-page, bound brochure produced in large print. It contains similar information to the above publication and is available form the same sources.

• "Yosemite Guide" is a bound newspaper tabloid (24 pages) which is issued seasonally. It contains general information about what to do and see in the park, general information and safety tips. Programs deemed "accessible with assistance" are highlighted by the international symbol of accessibility. It is available at the entrance and at information stations or by writing to the park.

Transportation

• Private vehicles may be used for transportation into the park and for travel *on roads designated for public use.*

• The National Park Service provides identifying placards for visitors with mobility impairments. These are available at entrance stations and at visitor centers. Parking in locations designated for visitors with disabilities requires the use of an identifying placard placed in the front windshield (visitors may use their own placard or the Park Service's) or valid "disabled person license plate". Other vehicles will be ticketed or towed.

• Visitors displaying the National Park Service "disabled person placard" are permitted to drive their vehicles on the Mirror Lake/Happy Isles Loop, a road otherwise closed to private vehicles. Visitors should check park literature for cautionary information.

• A free shuttle bus system, operated by the Yosemite Park and Curry Company, serves the eastern half of Yosemite Valley. Currently, three of the ten buses are equipped with front door wheelchair lifts and tie-downs for two wheelchairs. Others have a 12-inch step with handrail available. Buses run a regularly scheduled route. Bus stops include the following areas: Yosemite Lodge, the Ahwahnee, Curry Village, Campgrounds in the Valley, Yosemite Village, Yosemite Stables, Badger Pass Ski Area, Mariposa Big Trees, Glacier Point and Valley Visitor Center. The surfaces of the bus stops are reported to be level and smooth. The transportation staff has had experience serving visitors with a wide range of disabilities.

Sign Language Interpreter

• A skilled sign language interpreter is usually available during the summer season in Yosemite Valley. (See also *Organized Programs*, below.) Visitors should check the ''Yosemite Guide'' for current availability and schedule.

• A number of organized programs may have a sign language interpreter present during summer programming. Locations include: the Valley Visitor Center, the Indian Village (behind the Valley Visitor Center), Yosemite Lodge Amphitheater, Lower Pines Campground Amphitheater and Tenaya Creek. (See also *Organized Programs*, below.) Sign language programming is scheduled on selected days only, so visitors should check at the Valley Visitor Center for current scheduling.

TDD

• There is a National Park Service TDD for incoming calls requesting park information. The number is (209) 372-4726.

• The Yosemite Park and Curry Company has a TDD for incoming calls to make reservations for their lodgings within the park. The number is (209) 255-8345.

• A TDD service for both outgoing and incoming calls is available for hotel guests and residents at the Curry Village Registration Office. The number is (800) 855-1155.

Dog Guides

Dog guides may be used by visitors in the routine course of visiting park features and programs. Such dogs are also allowed in the back country and on trails, on shuttle buses and in Yosemite Park and Curry Company accommodations. They must be leashed at all times.

Programs

Organized Programs

• The Yosemite Orientation Program is a spectacular, wide-screen slide show, providing an overview of the park's resources and recreational opportunities. It is located at the West Auditorium of the **Valley Visitor Center**. (See *Visitor Center* section below for access information.) Captioning for visitors with hearing impairments is available by visitor request to the ranger in the Visitor Center. The program script is also available. The Visitor Center and Auditorium are reported to be accessible to wheelchair users with assistance. A sign language interpreter is frequently available at the Valley Visitor Center (Wednesdays through Sundays during summer). Restrooms adjacent to the Valley Visitor Center are usable. (See *Visitor Center* section.)

• Organized programs change with the season; visitors should consult the ''Yosemite Guide''. Special interpretive programs for organized groups are available on request and may be arranged through the group programs coordinator, phone (209) 372-4461, ext. 297. The listings which follow are typical offerings in the area of general ongoing programming.

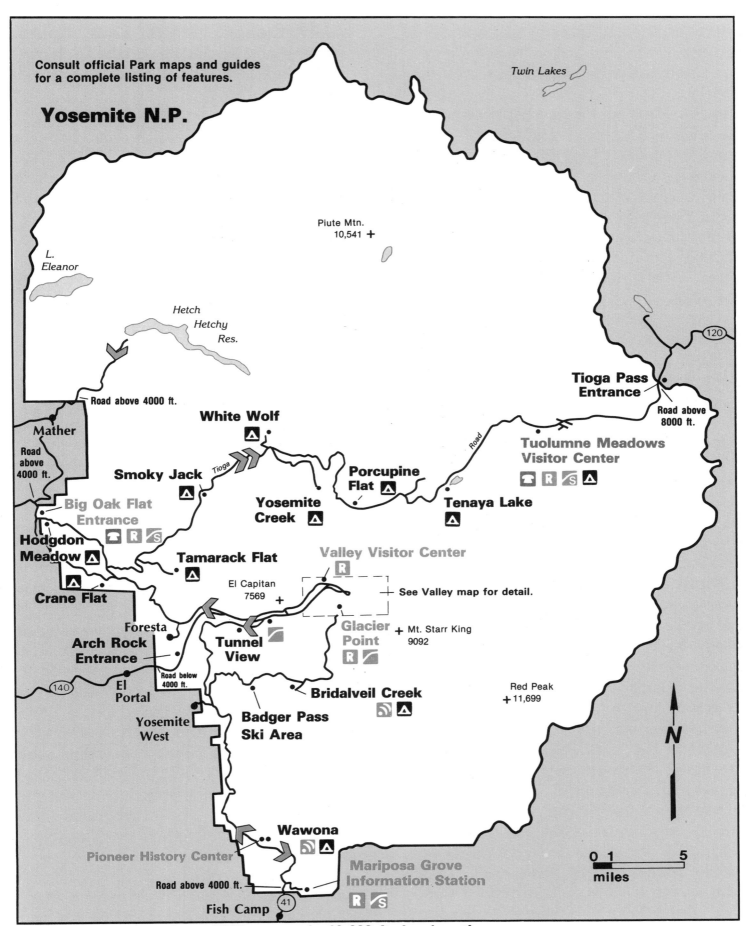

Consult official Park maps and guides for a complete listing of features.

Yosemite N.P.

Twin Lakes

Piute Mtn. 10,541 +

L. Eleanor

Hetch Hetchy Res.

120

Tioga Pass Entrance

Road above 8000 ft.

Road above 4000 ft.

Mather

Road above 4000 ft.

White Wolf

Tuolumne Meadows Visitor Center

Smoky Jack

Tioga

Porcupine Flat

Yosemite Creek

Tenaya Lake

Big Oak Flat Entrance

Hodgdon Meadow

Tamarack Flat

Valley Visitor Center

R

Crane Flat

El Capitan 7569 +

See Valley map for detail.

Foresta

Arch Rock Entrance

Tunnel View

Glacier Point

+ Mt. Starr King 9092

140

Road below 4000 ft.

El Portal

Bridalveil Creek

Red Peak + 11,699

Yosemite West

Badger Pass Ski Area

N

Wawona

Pioneer History Center

Mariposa Grove Information Station

Road above 4000 ft.

0 1   5
miles

41

Fish Camp

Park roads range from 3900 to nearly 10,000 ft. in elevation.

• Yosemite Theater, held in the **Valley Visitor Center** Auditorium, features programs of the performing arts and films about the park environment. (See *the Visitor Centers* section for access information.)

• **Indian Village**, located behind the Valley Visitor Center, re-creates the traditional village life of the Miwok and Paiute people of Yosemite. The Village is accessible to wheelchair users.

• The **Yosemite Museum** is located next to the Valley Visitor Center. The first floor of the Museum is accessible to wheelchair users. The Indian Cultural Exhibit describes the Ahwaneeche culture. Numerous basket and beadwork pieces are displayed with large-type labels. The Museum also houses the Fine Arts Gallery which exhibits selected pieces of artwork from the Park's archival collection of fine oil paintings, watercolors and photographs. The Park's Research Library is located on the second floor and is not accessible to wheelchair users.

• A two-hour bird walk originates at the **Valley Visitor Center**. It is reported to be accessible to wheelchair users with assistance.

• **Happy Isles Nature Center** contains exhibits, a children's corner, information and book sales. The Center is located two miles east of the Valley Visitor Center and is accessible by vehicle, the free Valley Shuttle Bus or via the bikeway. The Center is reported to be accessible to wheelchair users via ramp from the walk paralleling the river. Assistance may be necessary. Restrooms located at the shuttle bus stop are reported to be accessible.

• Evening ranger programs are reported to be accessible to wheelchair users with assistance. Programs are conducted at: **Valley Visitor Center, Bridalveil Creek Campground Amphitheater, Crane Flat Campground** (campfire circle), **Lower River Campground Amphitheater, Lower Pines Campground Am-** phitheater, **Tuolumne Meadows Campground, Wawona Campground Amphitheater, White Wolf Campground** and **Yosemite Lodge**. Scheduling changes seasonally, so visitors should check the Yosemite Guide for current events.

• A ranger-led walk, "A First Look at Yosemite", originates at the **Valley Visitor Center** and introduces the visitor to the scenery, stories and values of the Yosemite Valley. One-and-a-half hours in duration, it is reported to be accessible to wheelchair users with assistance. Similarly, a number of ranger-led nature walks ("Yosemite's Trees", "Yosemite's Indians", etc.), start at Valley Visitor Center and run for one-and-a-half to two hours. Many are reported to be accessible to wheelchair users with assistance.

• The **Art Activity Center** is located in Yosemite Valley. The facility is accessible. Free art lessons are available daily. No special programs are available for visitors with disabilities.

• "Sunset at Glacier Point" and "Full Moon at Glacier Point" are ranger-led programs focusing on the spectacular scenery. It meets at the railing at **Glacier Point**. Visitors should check times and schedule. A trail to Glacier Point is reported to be accessible to wheelchair users. Assistance may be needed. The restroom in the parking lot is reported to be accessible.

• Living history demonstrations and ranger-led tours are conducted at the **Pioneer Yosemite History Center** in the **Wawona** area. A one-hour film on bears is shown in the same area. It meets at the Artist's Cabin. Both programs are reported to be accessible to wheelchair users with assistance.

• A number of organized programs may have a sign language interpreter present during summer programming. In the past these have included: "A First Look at Yosemite", at the **Valley Visitor Center**;

Yosemite Valley

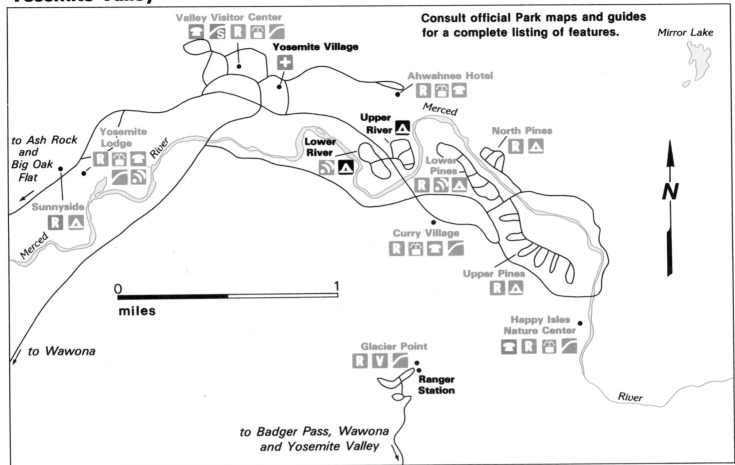

"Tow-Low-Yeht-Me-Wah" (Listen to the Indians), at the **Indian Village** behind the Valley Visitor Center; "At Day's End", a ranger-led walk meeting at the **Yosemite Lodge Amphitheater**, and evening programs conducted at **Lower Pines Campground Amphitheater** and the Yosemite Lodge Amphitheater. All are reported to be accessible to wheelchair users with assistance. Sign language programming is scheduled on selected days only, so visitors should check for current scheduling.

• The Information Station at **Big Oak Flat** furnishes orientation, trail information, wilderness permits, books and maps. The restroom and the Station are reported to be accessible to wheelchair users. Assistance may be necessary.

• The Visitor Center at **Tuolumne Meadows** is reported to be accessible. (See *Visitor Centers* section below.) Parking lot restrooms are reported to be accessible to wheelchair users.

Self-Guided Programs

• A short, self-guiding trail, located behind the Valley Visitor Center, passes through the **Indian Garden**, a reconstructed Miwok/Paiute village. It is accessible to wheelchair users. This concrete walk is marked with interpretive signs and a large-print brochure is available.

• A self-guiding nature trail, "A Changing Yosemite" begins near the **Valley Visitor Center**, Shuttle Bus Stop #6. Trail pamphlets may be picked up at the Visitor Center or at the sign at the trailhead. The trail is one-mile-long paved walkway that is accessible.

• Some of the Giant Sequoias of **Mariposa Grove** can be seen in the immediate vicinity of the parking area, reported to be accessible. A tram serves the Mariposa Grove area. Though it is not accessible to wheelchair users, visitors with disabilities are permitted to drive their own vehicle through the Grove and are loaned a tape player with an interpretive message by the

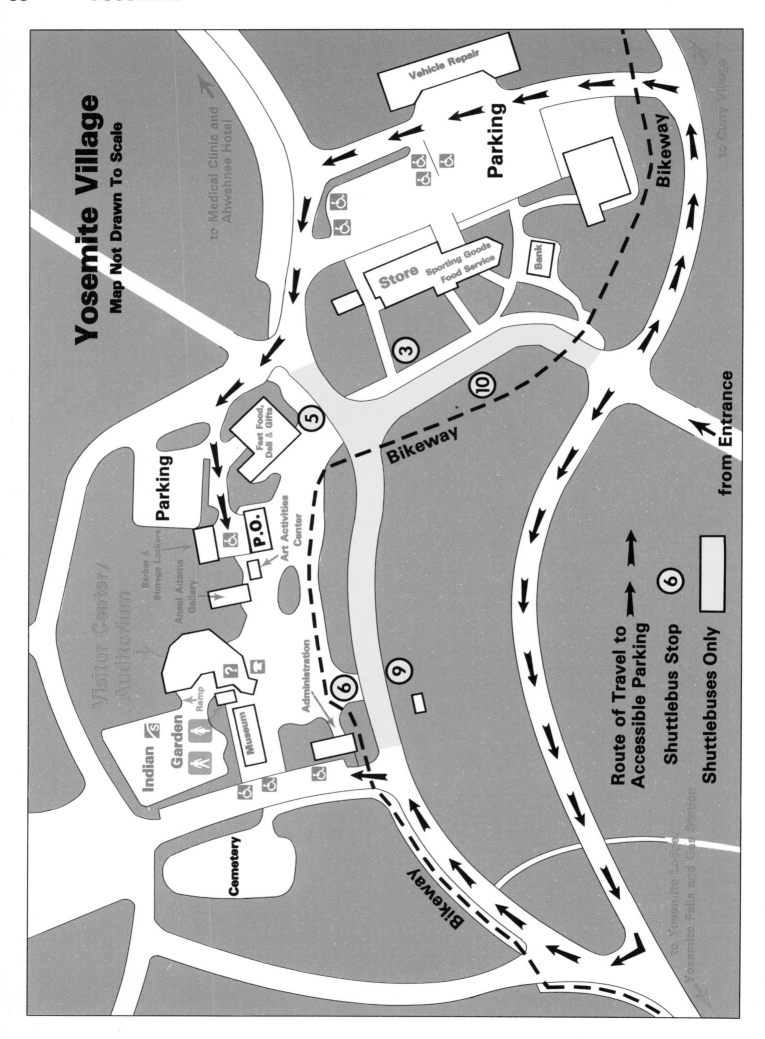

tram dispatcher. The tram dispatcher, summoned by the visitor's horn, will open the gate. There is an accessible unisex restroom in the parking lot. Request the key at the tram ticket kiosk.

• A self-guiding trail through the Tuolumne Grove of the Giant Sequoias is one-half mile long. The trail is not fully accessible to wheelchair users and is characterized as "moderately difficult". The trailhead is one mile down the Tuolumne Grove Road from **Crane Flat** junction at the nature trail parking area.

• At **Tuolumne Meadows** there is a self-guiding trail to Soda Springs and Parsons Memorial Lodge. The trailhead is a quarter-mile along the road to the Tuolumne Meadows Stables. This trail is not fully accessible to wheelchair users as it has a sand and gravel surface. The trail is one mile long. There is no shuttle bus stop here.

• "Yosemite Road Guide", designed for use by all visitors, is an 80-page brochure that offers interpretation of many of the park's features and roadside attractions. The brochure contents are keyed to numbered roadside markers. It is for sale at the visitor centers, entrance stations and most park gift shops.

Trails

The following trails are reported to be accessible to wheelchair users with assistance:

• Lower Yosemite Falls - The trail starts at Yosemite Falls Shuttle Stop. It is 500 yards round trip. The last 30 yards has steep grades (7% to 10%). A unisex restroom located at the parking lot is reported to be accessible.

• **Bridalveil Falls** - The trail starts at the southeast corner of the parking area. It is 100 yards round trip. The first 30 yards has 2% to 4% gradient. The last 20 yards will require assistance with a grade of 7% to 10%. There is no accessible restroom.

• Mirror Lake Trail - This trail is a road closed to traffic and used primarily by horses. Visitors with the disabled person placard are allowed to drive their private vehicles on this road (called the Mirror Lake/Happy Isles Loop). Visitors with disabilities who wish to walk or wheel the road should evaluate the potential with a park ranger.

• Old Road along the base of El Capitan - The trail starts at a dirt parking space at the west end of El Capitan Meadow. It is 300 yards round trip. Maximum grade is 3%. The trail (an abandoned paved road) is bumpy and may be strewn with sand and pine needles and cones.

• A trail which is reported to be accessible leads to a wetland west of the **Happy Isles Nature Center**. The wetland is an excellent area for birding. The trail runs from the food concession, north of the Nature Center, to the wetland. It is approximately 300 yards long. It may be accessed either near the food concession or from a designated, reserved parking area on the service road running south from shutttlebus stop #16.

• **Yosemite Lodge** to **Curry Village** Trail - This trail is "easy" with a 1% to 3% maximum grade. The distance is 2 miles one-way. This is a bicycle path so users should be aware of bicyclists and keep to the right of the centerline.

Exhibits

• In general, exhibits are reported to have adjacent clear space and are at appropriate heights to be accessible to wheelchair users.

• Most exhibit signs employ high-contrast lettering. Non-glare glass is used, and most exhibits are well-lighted.

• A three-dimensional exhibit describing how glaciers carved Yosemite Valley is located at the Valley Visitor Center. This exhibit may be touched.

• A plaster map of Yosemite Valley is located at the **Happy Isles Nature Center**. This exhibit may be touched.

Visitor Centers

Yosemite Valley Visitor Center

• Located at the west end of Yosemite Village. It is open daily.

• Parking for the Visitor Center is located near the Administration Building. Three spaces are reserved, signed and accessible. There are no curbs. (See the Yosemite Village inset map for location of close-in parking.) Overnight visitors should consider using the free shuttle bus from their motel or campsite. *Note: Visitors with disabilities are not permitted to drive or park on the pedestrian mall in front of the Visitor Center.*

• The main walkway in front of the Visitor Center is wide and smooth with a gentle 3% slope. There is a five-foot level platform area in front of the doorway. The doorway is 36 inches wide. The door is heavy and may be difficult to use. Assistance may be needed.

• The information desk and sales area are accessible. The display and exhibit area has a sloping floor. Access to this area will require assistance.

• Two auditoriums, known as the East and West Auditoriums, are located behind the information and exhibit area of the Visitor Center. During the day when the exhibit area is open, the auditoriums may be reached by exiting the exhibit area into an outdoor courtyard. In the evening, when the exhibit area is closed, the courtyard can be reached via a walkway on the left side of the Visitor Center. An accessible ramp leads to the auditorium entrances. The doorways are 36 inches wide.

• Restrooms are located in a separate building between the Visitor Center and the Indian Museum. They are reported to be accessible. They have large stalls designed for wheelchair users. Grab bars are one inch in diameter.

• A water fountain located near the restrooms is reported to be accessible.

• A telephone which is accessible to wheelchair users is located outside the Visitor Center. It may not have volume control or be hearing-aid compatible.

Tuolumne Meadows Visitor Center

• Open spring through fall.

• Visitors with disabilities may drive through the parking lot and up the service road. A signed, reserved parking space is located on the west (right) side of the building.

• From the reserved parking, visitors should proceed past the main entrance to the opposite end of the building. There an accessible ramp leads to an alternate entrance. The building is reported to be accessible.

• A permanent accessible ramp leads to temporary restrooms located in the parking area during the summer season. These restrooms are reported to be accessible.

• A unisex restroom, reported to be accessible, is located at the Tuolumne Store/Grill, one-half mile east.

• The telephone in the Visitor Center is not accessible. A telephone which is accessible to wheelchair users is at the nearby Ranger Station. It may not have volume control or be hearing-aid compatible.

Happy Isles Nature Center

• The Nature Center is reported to be accessible. The entrance is via a ramp from the walk paralleling the river. The restroom and water fountain at the shuttle bus stop are reported to be accessible.

• A telephone which is accessible to wheelchair users is located outside the Nature Center, on the blacktop sidewalk. (This telephone's location is not readily evident; visitors should inquire inside Nature Center.) It may not have volume control or be hearing-aid compatible.

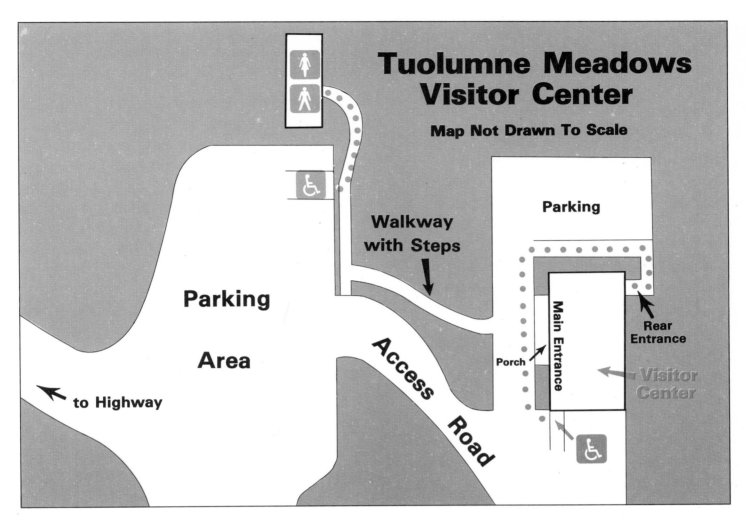

Big Oak Flat Information Station

• The information station and restroom are both reported to be accessible.

• A telephone which is accessible to wheelchair users is located inside the Visitor Center. It may not have volume control or be hearing-aid compatible.

Campgrounds

Note: Reservations are required for campgrounds in Yosemite Valley during the spring, summer and fall. Reservations must be made through Ticketron®. To reserve a designated site (in Lower or Upper Pines Campground), such request must be made. Apply in person at any local Ticketron® office or by mail to:

Ticketron®
Department R
401 Hackensack Ave.
Hackensack, NJ 07601

Lower Pines Campground

The first loop of this campground has been designated for use by visitors with disabilities. There are asphalt pathways. Restrooms have a large stall which allows for side transfer from a wheelchair. Electrical outlets are available in the restroom. All sites in this loop are reported to be level; however, only two sites have tables with extended tops.

Upper Pines Campground

One site in the first loop of this campground has a designated site. The site has an extended-top picnic table. This loop has asphalt pathways and a restroom with a large stall which allows for side transfer from a wheelchair. Electrical outlets are available in the restroom.

North Pines Group Campground

Reservations for the Group Campground may be made by mail or by calling (209) 372-4461, extension 240 or 224. Vehicles may be driven to the site for unloading of passengers and equipment but must be parked in the designated parking spaces in the North Pines Campground (N.P.S. "disabled person" placard must be displayed). One restroom is reported to be accessible.

Sunnyside Walk-In Campground

This campground has no accessible sites but many sites are level; two sites have accessible tables. The restroom has two accessible unisex toilets. Parking is available in a lot adjacent to the ranger kiosk about 100 yards from the restroom.

Other Campgrounds

Wawona, Bridalveil Creek, Crane Flat, Hodgdon Meadow, Tamarack Flat, Smokey Jack, White Wolf, Yosemite Creek, Porcupine Flat and Tuolumne Meadows Campgrounds have no campsites that have been designed specifically or are especially appropriate for visitors with disabilities.

Supplementary Information

• Several facilities in Yosemite Valley are reported by the Park to be accessible as follows:

National Park Service Headquarters - The Superintendent's Office and Personnel Office are located on the ground floor which is accessible.

U.S. Post Office - accessible via the door at the west end.

Degnons - The deli, gift shop and "fast foods" are located on the ground floor which is accessible.

Barber shop, storage lockers and **restrooms** - accessible.

The Village Store - accessible.

A hamburger stand and **sporting goods shop** are accessible.

Bank of America - The Versiteller function located on the entrance deck is accessible.

Concession Headquarters - accessible.

Photo Processing - accessible.
Vehicle Repair - accessible.

• **Yosemite Dental Clinic** is located in Yosemite Valley. It is fully accessible to wheelchair users via the Emergency/Ambulance entrance at the back entrance to the building. There is designated, reserved parking on a blacktop surface. The staff is experienced serving clients with a variety of disabilities including visual, hearing and mobility impairments.

• **Yosemite Park and Curry Company** (Yosemite National Park, California 95389) runs the following concessions. Telephone (209) 372-1000; there is also TDD service at (209) 255-8345 for incoming calls to make lodging reservations. Reservations for hotels or lodges can be made up to one year in advance. Reservations may be obtained by writing to:

Yosemite Reservations
541 East Home Ave.
Fresno, CA 93727

The Ahwahnee Hotel - The staff has had experience at serving guests with a wide range of disabilities, including those with special medical needs. The staff has been sensitized to the needs of visitors with disabilities. The Hotel is receptive to hosting small groups of visitors with developmental disabilities if special reservations are made in advance.

There is signed, reserved, level parking on an asphalt surface. (A "California Handicap Sticker", N.P.S. placard, or valid "disabled person license plate" is required.) Parking is located 60 feet from the hotel entrance. The passenger loading zone is a level, smooth, wooden surface. If necessary, the staff will assist guests in disembarking from a vehicle and entering the facility. The route of travel from the parking/passenger loading zone is reported to be accessible.

Registration is done by card. A clipboard is available on request. Pre-registration, if convenient for the guest, may be done by mail or telephone. The staff will assist with registration if necessary.

Access to rooms is by means of a ramp with a gradient less than 1:12. The ramp is three feet wide and has a non-slip surface but lacks edging. An elevator is in use and is reported to meet UFAS or ANSI standards. There are no braille operating controls but floor levels are announced by loud speaker. If necessary, the staff will assist guests in getting to rooms. Two rooms (two beds each) have been specifically designed and modified to accommodate guests with disabilities and are fully accessible, containing bathrooms and shower stalls. Advanced reservations are required. A six- to twelve-month lead time may be necessary.

Unisex, communal bathrooms are located on the mezzanine and are reported to be accessible. The swimming pool is located on an accessible route from the lodging area. Telephones and a water fountain are reported to be on an accessible route and positioned low enough for operation by wheelchair users.

The Ahwahnee Hotel dining room is reported accessible. The dining room staff has had experience in serving guests with a wide range of disabilities and is willing to assist with guests' needs. Unisex restroom facilities are present and reported to be specifically designed for accessibility.

Curry Village - The staff has had experience at serving guests with a wide range of disabilities, including those with special medical needs. The staff has been sensitized to the needs of visitors with disabilities. The Hotel is receptive to hosting small groups of visitors with developmental disabilities. No special reservations need be made in advance.

There is signed, reserved, level parking on an asphalt surface. (A local Disabled Motorist Vehicle sticker, N.P.S. placard or valid "disabled person license plate" is required.) Parking is located ten feet to two hundred yards from the Curry Village entrance. The parking area surface varies from blacktop to sand and gravel. The passenger loading zone is level, smooth, blacktop with wooden walkways. It is located adjacent to the motel registration area. If necessary, the staff will assist guests in disembarking from a vehicle and entering the facility. The route of travel from the parking and passenger loading zone is reported accessible by means of a wooden walkway and ramp. The ramp is three feet wide with a gradient less than 1:12.

Registration is done by card with a clipboard available on request. Pre-registration, if convenient for the guest, may be done by mail or telephone. The staff will assist with registration if necessary.

Access to rooms is by means of a relatively rough walkway with a surface composed of wood, sand and "etc." and a ramp with a gradient in excess of 1:12. The ramp is three feet wide, has edging and hand rails but does not have an all-weather, non-slip surface. If necessary, the staff will assist guests in getting to rooms. Two rooms (two beds each) have been specifically designed and modified to accommodate guests with disabilities and are fully accessible, containing bathrooms and shower stalls. Advanced reservations are required. A lead time of one year may be necessary.

Communal bathroom facilities (3 men, 3 women) are located around the complex and are reported to be accessible. The swimming pool is accessed by dirt paths; assistance may be required. Telephones and a water fountain are reported to be on an accessible route and positioned low enough for operation by wheelchair users.

Food services in the Village are located in the cafeteria, hamburger stand, pizza stand, ice cream stand and bar. The staff has had experience serving guests with a wide range of disabilities and is willing to assist with guests' needs. Restrooms serving the food service areas are reported to be accessible.

Note: A TDD service for both outgoing and incoming calls is available at the Curry Village Registration Office for hotel guests and residents. The number is (800) 855-1155.

Hotel Wawona - This hotel is over one hundred years old and lack of accessibility reflects this. The staff has had experience at serving guests who are wheelchair users and visitors with developmental disabilities. The staff has been sensitized to the needs of visitors with disabilities. The Hotel is receptive to hosting small groups of visitors with developmental disabilities. No special reservations are needed.

There is no reserved parking. The parking area is reported to be level, smooth asphalt. The passenger loading zone is a level, smooth, asphalt surface which is located about 20 feet from the hotel entrance. If necessary, the staff will assist guests in disembarking from a vehicle and entering the facility. The route of travel from the parking and passenger loading zone does not meet accessibility standards.

Registration is done by card, with a clipboard available on request. Pre-registration is not possible. The staff will assist with registration if necessary.

Access to rooms does not meet accessibility standards. Two hotel rooms have ramped access but no further modifications have been made. Door widths, including in-room bathrooms, are reported to range from 32 to 36 inches. Advanced reservations are required. A one-year lead time may be necessary.

Communal bathrooms are not accessi-

NATIONAL PARK SERVICE

ble to wheelchair users. The swimming pool, tennis court and golf course are reported to be located on an accessible route from lodging sites. Telephones and a water fountain are reported to be on an accessible route and positioned low enough for operation by wheelchair users.

The food service area (dining room) is reported accessible. The route of travel is concrete and astro-turf. The dining room staff has had experience serving guests with a wide range of disabilities and is willing to assist with guests' needs. The restroom in the dining area is reported to be on an accessible route and to have a door width of 36 inches. No other modifications are in place; stalls and turning spaces may be too narrow for wheelchair users.

Tuolumne Meadows Lodge - This lodge is not readily accessible to wheelchair users. Lodging is in canvas tents in a mountainous, alpine setting. The staff is willing to assist but visitors with disabilities should inquire regarding details.

White Wolf Lodge - This lodge is not readily accessible to wheelchair users. Lodging is in canvas tents in a mountainous, alpine setting. The staff is willing to assist but visitors with disabilities should inquire regarding details.

Yosemite Lodge - The staff has had experience serving guests with a wide range of disabilities, including those with special medical needs. The staff has been sensitized to the needs of visitors with disabilities. Assuming adequate supervision by accompanying caregivers, the Lodge is receptive to hosting small groups of visitors with developmental disabilities if special reservations are made in advance.

There is signed, reserved, level parking on an asphalt surface. (A "Disabled Motorist Vehicle" sticker, N.P.S. placard or valid "disabled person license plate" is required.) The parking is located 50 feet from the Lodge entrance. The passenger loading zone is a level, smooth, asphalt surface located 50 feet from the lodge entrance. If necessary, the staff will assist guests in disembarking from a vehicle and entering the facility. The route of travel from the parking and passenger loading zone to the lodge entrance is reported to be accessible over a concrete surface and a permanent ramp. The ramp is four feet wide and has no edging.

Registration is done by card with a clipboard available on request. Pre-registration, if convenient for the guest, may be done by mail or telephone. The staff will assist with registration if necessary.

Access to rooms is by means of an asphalt walkway that may be bumpy; assistance may be required. Nineteen rooms (two beds each) have been specifically designed and modified to accommodate guests with disabilities and are reported to be accessible. Clear spaces between furniture elements may be tight; door controls are lever-operated from the inside, knob on outside. The telephone is not accessible from the bed. Bathrooms have 32-inch door widths. The shower stalls and bathroom facilities are reported accessible. The hot water pipes, however, are not insulated. Advanced reservations are required. A one-year lead time may be necessary.

The swimming pool is located on an smooth pathway about 200 yards from the lodging; assistance may be required. Telephones and water fountain are reported to be on an accessible route and positioned low enough for operation by wheelchair users. The cafeteria, Four Seasons Restaurant, Mountain Broiler Room and Mountain Room Bar are reported to be accessible. The food service staff has had experience serving guests with a wide range of disabilities and is willing to assist with guests' needs. Restrooms are located in the cafeteria and at the restaurant entrance; both have been modified for use by guests with disabilities but may not meet all UFAS or ANSI standards.

The Ansel Adams Gallery (gift shop) - The staff is experienced in serving visitors with a wide range of disabilities and has been sensitized to their needs and willing to assist them.

The concession is located about 100 yards from reserved parking. The building has two levels. A permanent ramp located at the side of the building provides wheelchair access to the first level. The ramp is wider than 36 inches and has an all-weather, non-slip surface but no edging or handrails. The ramp grade is less than 1:12.

Aisles in sales area are at least 36 inches wide and are kept free of displays and inventory. Maximum shelf height is seven feet. The checkout counter is located between 24 and 34 inches above the floor. The checkout aisle is at least 36 inches wide. No restrooms are available.

Yosemite Park And Curry Company Rafting (self-guided raft trips) - Use of these services is currently restricted to individuals capable of paddling, swimming and making clear judgment decisions. The staff has been sensitized to the needs of visitors with disabilities. Visitors with mobility impairments must be accompanied by an "able-bodied" companion. Children with mild developmental disabilities are permitted access when accompanied by responsible adults. The concession has had successful experiences with visitors with hearing disabilities, developmental disabilities and special medical needs.

Yosemite Stables (horseback riding) - Because of perceived danger, the concession has restricted use. This activity is not recommended for visitors with "severe physical disabilities". The staff has no experience serving visitors with disabilities.

Basic Facilities

	Restroom	Water Fountain	Telephone
Ahwahnee Hotel	●	●	●
Big Oak Flat Information Station	●		●
Curry Village	●	●	●
Glacier Point	●		
Happy Isles Nature Center	●	●	●
Lower Pines Campground	●		
Mariposa Grove	●		
North Pines Campground	●		
Sunnyside Campground	●		
Tuolumne Meadows Visitor Center	●		●
Upper Pines Campground	●		
Valley Visitor Center	●	●	●
Yosemite Lodge	●	●	●

There are three volume control phones available in Yosemite Valley. They are located: 1) behind the Village Store, 2) in the Yosemite Lodge Building and 3) at Curry Village. Telephones located at the Park's four entrance gates (South Entrance, Arch Rock, Tioga Pass and Big Oak Flat) are accessible to wheelchair users. These phones may not have volume control or be hearing-aid compatible.